SYRIA
Modern State in an Ancient Land

John F. Devlin

Profiles / Nations of the Contemporary Middle East

SYRIA

SYRIA

Modern State in an Ancient Land

John F. Devlin

Westview Press • Boulder, Colorado

Croom Helm • London, England

Profiles/Nations of the Contemporary Middle East

Photo credits: Pages 73 and 85 (top), author's photos; page 115, United Press International, Inc. All other photos courtesy of the Syrian Embassy, Washington, D.C.

Jacket and paperback cover photos: (top left) modern Damascus; (top right) old water wheel at Hama; (lower left) dam on Euphrates nearing completion; (lower right) traditional pastoral scene. All photos courtesy of Syrian Embassy except water wheel (author's photo).

Published in 1983 in the United States of America by
  Westview Press, Inc.
  5500 Central Avenue
  Boulder, Colorado 80301
  Frederick A. Praeger, President and Publisher

Published in 1983 in Great Britain by
  Croom Helm Ltd.
  Provident House
  Burrell Row
  Beckenham, Kent BR3 1AT

Library of Congress Catalog Card Number: 82-15909
ISBN (U.S.): 0-86531-185-4
ISBN(U.K.): 0-7099-0831-8

Printed and bound in the United States of America

In memory of a wise and good

and gallant woman,

R.V.D.

Contents

Illustrations

Acknowledgments

Although the responsibility for a book is the author's alone, he inevitably owes much to others. In the first place are the dozens of persons with whom I have, over the years, discussed Middle Eastern affairs and Syria in particular, whose views, opinions, and queries have helped sharpen my perceptions. I have benefited from the analytical work of those who study contemporary Syria, notably Raymond Hinnebusch, Michael Van Dusen, Alasdair Drysdale, Patrick Seale, Nikolaos van Dam, Hanna Batatu, Robert Olson, Robert Springborg, and Itamar Rabinovich, although in a work such as this direct citations are few.

Special thanks go to my friends and colleagues: Gordon Torrey, who generously gave me free run of his library, and Earnest Oney, whose careful reading of the manuscript greatly improved its historical accuracy. Last, but surely not least, I express appreciation to Bobbie Church and Susan Kelly, who at divers times typed portions of the manuscript.

John F. Devlin
Swarthmore, Pennsylvania

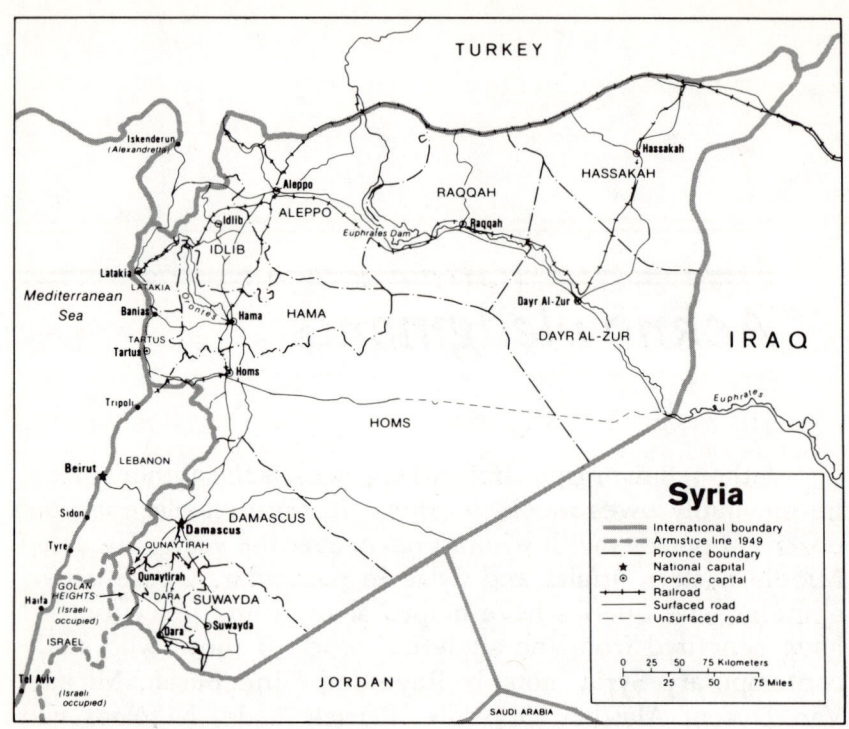

Syria

- ━━━ International boundary
- ═══ Armistice line 1949
- ─ ·· ─ Province boundary
- ★ National capital
- ⊛ Province capital
- ✛━✛ Railroad
- ━━━ Surfaced road
- ─ ─ ─ Unsurfaced road

| 0 | 25 | 50 | 75 Kilometers |
| 0 | 25 | 50 | 75 Miles |

TURKEY

Iskenderun
(Alexandretta)

Hassakah

RAQQAH

HASSAKAH

Aleppo
ALEPPO

Idlib

IDLIB

Raqqah

Euphrates Dam

Latakia
LATAKIA

Banias

Hama

HAMA

Dayr Al-Zur

DAYR AL-ZUR

IRAQ

Mediterranean
Sea

Orontes

TARTUS
Tartus

Homs

Euphrates

Tripoli

HOMS

Beirut

LEBANON

DAMASCUS

Sidon

Damascus

Tyre

QUNAYTIRAH

Qunaytirah

Haifa

GOLAN
HEIGHTS
(Israeli
occupied)

DARA

SUWAYDA

ISRAEL

Dara

Suwayda

Tal Aviv

(Israeli
occupied)

JORDAN

SAUDI ARABIA

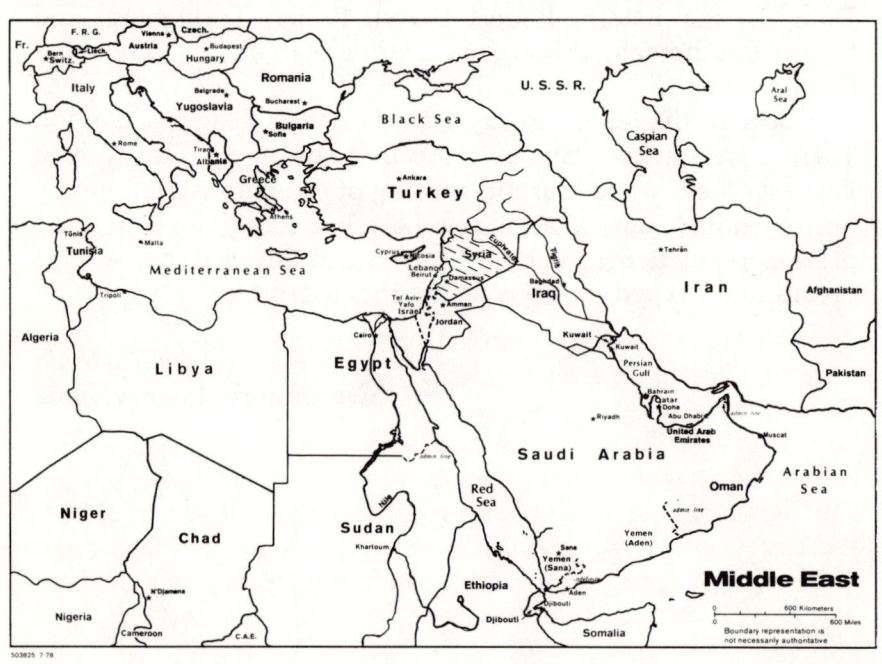

Middle East

Fr.
F.R.G.
Vienna
Czech.
Bern
Switz.
Austria
Budapest
Hungary
Italy
Belgrade
Yugoslavia
Romania
Bucharest
Bulgaria
Sofia
Rome
Tirana
Albania
Greece
Athens
Tunis
Tunisia
Malta
Tripoli
Mediterranean Sea

Black Sea

Ankara
Turkey

U.S.S.R.

Aral
Sea

Caspian
Sea

Cyprus
Nicosia
Lebanon
Beirut
Syria
Tel Aviv
Yafo
Israel
Damascus
Amman
Jordan
Cairo

Euphrates
Tigris

Baghdad
Iraq

Kuwait
Kuwait

Tehrān

Iran

Afghanistan

Pakistan

Algeria

Libya

Egypt

Red
Sea

Saudi Arabia

Riyadh

Bahrain
Qatar
Doha
Abu Dhabi
United Arab
Emirates

Persian
Gulf

Muscat

Oman

Arabian
Sea

Niger

Chad

N'Djamena

Sudan

Khartoum

Ethiopia

Djibouti

Sana
Yemen
(Sana)

Yemen
(Aden)

Aden line

Somalia

Nigeria

Cameroon

C.A.E.

Boundary representation is
not necessarily authoritative

| 0 | 600 Kilometers |
| 0 | 600 Miles |

503825 7-78

1

Introduction

The Syrian Arab Republic is at one and the same time the product of forces and events peculiar to the twentieth century and the heir to a past that reaches back to antiquity. Predominantly mainstream Muslim in population, the country has lived under a secular ideology more than half its independent life. Because of historical, geographical, and cultural factors, Syrians have, over the thirty-five years of the country's independent existence, variously looked on the Arab nation, an enlarged Syria, the present republic, their religious sect, or their district as the proper field of political life. The question of what a Syrian's primary identity should be runs through the nation's contemporary history. And the answer affects the legitimacy of various groups that have claimed the right to run the state.

The story of this country, which became independent in 1946, is one of a state whose terms of existence were established by outsiders, primarily Europeans. For three and a half decades Syrians have been caught up in the process of adjusting to, modifying, or overturning those terms. The process has been convulsive; the coup d'etat was for a time considered to be an integral element in governing the country. Some issues have been settled, some are partially so, and others are still open, as the following chapters will discuss.

That a newly independent state should go through a tumultuous and stressful time is the norm rather than the exception. The Syrian people had to learn to govern themselves, to choose the system under which they were willing to live, and to accept one leader or group or point of view and reject another. Syrians had a wide range of choices in a period in which traditional ways of doing things came under challenge from within and without the country. Using choice in that way implies that Syrians were able to examine a spectrum of competing ideas and systems laid out like goods on a counter and pick the model that most appealed to them. In a way, that has been true. France, as mandatory power after World War I, introduced the forms of representative democracy, which contrasted sharply with the authoritarian cast of previous Ottoman rule. Communism was introduced in the 1930s; variations of socialism came in as well. Movements modeled on European fascist examples appeared. All competed with the traditional dominance of a wealthy merchant-landowner class and with homegrown political ideas.

In another sense, the opportunity afforded the Syrian people to choose the politico-economic system they wanted was far from clearcut. The choice was made piecemeal through dozens of events, actions, and failures to take action by political leaders, businessmen, military officers, and others. Collectively, these elements have led to rule by the military establishment through the agency of the Baath party. Whether the process is finished, whether this form of government and society will prevail for the next few generations, is an open question, aspects of which will be addressed in the concluding chapter.

The process of choice both contributed to and was conditioned by the change that has characterized independent Syria. Since the start of World War II the population has grown from 2.5 million to 9 million. The cities alone now hold nearly twice as many people as did the whole country in 1938. Where there were scarcely four thousand motor vehicles in 1938, today the cities are crowded with cars. A largely illiterate society is being transformed into a lettered bureaucratic one. Farming is no longer the occupation of the vast majority of Syrians.

Syria in the 1980s is still changing. Some forces are pushing it in the direction of further modernization; others are resisting. There is disagreement as to who should govern. Differences over these matters have broken into violence during the last few years. All these factors indicate that Syria is not a static society but a dynamic one. The following chapters attempt to show how the country came to be what it is. They look at the influences that formed it and try to explain where it stands along the road of change from a conservative, traditional Middle Eastern Muslim society to a late-twentieth century, centralized bureaucratic state. Merely to describe Syria as it is today would be inadequate to explain it. The last chapter, in particular, looks at the issues that Syrians are grappling with in 1982 and that they will have to deal with in the years ahead. The purpose of that chapter is not to predict the future but to point out a number of key issues and likely events that will compel new choices from Syrians, set limits for them, and perhaps open new avenues of opportunity for this dynamic modern society rooted in an ancient land.

The name of that land has meant different things at various times. The modern Syrian Arab Republic—the Syria of this book—constitutes a part of the area customarily known as Syria until the early twentieth century. The larger area extends from the mountains that line the southern border of modern Turkey south to the edge of the Sinai and from the Mediterranean Sea to the desert. That area is called in this book "geographic Syria" to distinguish it from the Syrian Arab Republic.

2

The Past

It is a truism—perhaps trite but nonetheless apt—that a country grows out of the people who inhabit it, their past, and the physical nature of their surroundings. The land and its resources determine what people can do for their livelihood. Those same elements may attract others from outside, who may pillage and leave, conquer and rule from afar, or stay and become part of the essence. How the people relate to their physical surroundings, what they have done, and what has been done to them combine to create the present. Just as important as what happened is a people's perception of what happened—their national myth, so to speak. The pages that follow sketch the interplay of the elements that have gone into the making of the modern state of Syria.

EARLY HISTORY

The land that geographic Syria occupies has been populated since antiquity. Damascus, the capital, and Aleppo, the large northern commercial center, are contenders for the title of "oldest continuously inhabited city in the world." The alphabet was invented in geographic Syria during the second millenium B.C. Recent excavations at Ebla show a major state controlling substantial areas and trading and fighting with the long better-known civilizations of the Nile Valley in Egypt and the Tigris-Euphrates in Mesopotamia.

But Syria has often been under the sway of powers from outside. Three contiguous regions have been the homelands of powers that conquered, controlled, or influenced Syria from antiquity to modern times. The Egyptians, to the south, dominated

geographic Syria for a century in the second millenium, to be
followed by the Hittites, whose heartland lay to the north in
Asia Minor in what is now Turkey. The Assyrians from the
Tigris valley to the east swept into geographic Syria, coming
"down like a wolf on the fold" during the heyday of their power,
beginning around 1000 B.C., and ruled Syria for the better part of
two centuries. During Assyrian administration, Aramaic
became the common language of the area, a status it was to re-
tain long into the Christian era. Under the Persians, who incorporated Syria into their empire (which stretched from western
Asia Minor to the Hindu Kush mountains of modern
Afghanistan), Aramaic became the official language of the
region. The Israelites who were hauled off to Babylon by
Nebuchadnezzar in 597–596 B.C. – between the Assyrians and
the Persians, the Babylonians had a turn at dominating Syria
and Palestine – were familiar with it.

With the emergence of Alexander of Macedon, there began
a thousand-year period of domination of the eastern end of the
Mediterranean by powers based further to the west, Greece and
Rome. In the decade from 332 to 323 B.C., Alexander's armies
destroyed the Persian empire. Syria became the center of power
of the Seleucids, descendants of one of Alexander's generals, until the Romans took the area, just prior to the beginning of the
Christian era. They secured the bounds of their empire by a
series of forts linked by good roads, along a line that is roughly
congruent with the southeastern boundary of modern Syria.
The relics of Rome are still common in the area; with a passion
for organization and skill in engineering the Romans built roads,
bridges, hydraulic works, and temples with a solidity that has
defied centuries of neglect and theft and reuse of some of their
building materials. Following the division of the Roman Empire
into two states in the fourth century A.D., Syria fell under the
rule of Byzantium (Constantinople), the Eastern Roman Empire,
of which Asia Minor was the heart. The province's resources
were used for, and the area became a battleground in, a drawn-
out struggle between Byzantium and Persia. The struggle left
both empires severely weakened and unable to repel a powerful, indeed irresistible, challenge from Arabia early in the
seventh century.

THE SPREAD OF ISLAM

This last incursion brought to Syria, and to the entire Middle East, changes in language, religion, and culture that have endured to this day. The rise of Islam is the most important event in the formation of Syria. In A.D. 636, an army of devotees of the new faith defeated the Byzantine army and drove it north of the Taurus Mountains. It was not an easy victory; the losers fought skillfully and tenaciously, but the populace had grown weary of Byzantine rule and gave insufficient support to the imperial armies. The adherence of Syria to Muslim rule and culture has been permanent; the Taurus Mountains running east and west between what are today Syria and Turkey became, with temporary fluctuations and minor changes, the boundary between Christianity and Islam until Turkish invaders from the east, already converted to Islam, overran Asia Minor in the eleventh century.

Islam, today the religion of three-quarters of a billion people, had begun scarcely twenty-five years before the expulsion of the Byzantines from Syria. Early in the seventh century, Muhammad, a merchant of the western Arabian city of Mecca (A.D. 570–632) received the first of a series of revelations, which he and his followers, and all Muslims since, believed to have been given him directly by God. He was the Messenger, the one through whom God's design for man's salvation would finally and definitively be given to the world. For this was not, in the Muslims' belief, a new religion, but a correction of earlier transmissions of the message to the Jews through their prophets, Abraham, Moses, Elijah, and others, and again through Jesus; Muhammad taught that both Jews and Christians had distorted the message. Nonetheless, the Judeo-Christian tradition is respected by Muslims, and Jews and Christians are "people of the book," distinct from the common run of infidels, i.e., those who never received any portion of the divine revelation.

Islam—the word means submission to God (Allah in Arabic)—had and has the appeal of simplicity. Its doctrine is summed up in the profession, "There is no god but God, and Muhammad is his Messenger." The essential requirements for a Muslim, in addition to the profession of faith, are prayer in a prescribed fashion, fasting one month of the lunar year, alms-giving, and pilgrimage to the birthplace of Islam, the western Arabian city of Mecca, once in a lifetime for all able to make the journey. Because of its simplicity and no doubt because of the enthusiasm and power of its adherents, Islam spread with phenomenal speed. A century after Muhammad's death, Muslim rule extended from the Pyrenees in Spain across North Africa and the Middle East through Iran to central Asia. The conquest of Syria was merely a beginning. The Muslims brought with them the Arabic language, martial skill, and a new calendar—a lunar one—that started in 622 of the Christian era. In that year, because of opposition to his preaching, Muham-mad left Mecca and established himself and his followers in the neighboring city of Medina.

The message proclaimed by Muhammad envisaged a soci-ety in which religion, government, social conduct, and personal status were all of a piece. Separation of church and state and in-dividual choice in religious matters, which we have come to think of as normal in Western society, were and are alien to traditional Islam. The Quran and the traditions provide the believer with all the guidance he needs for life. Muhammad also envisaged a single Muslim state. His successor moved the gov-ernment to Syria, and for nearly a century (661–750) Damascus was the capital of that huge state, the Ummayyad Empire. Reminders of this period of glory exist in Damascus to this day, notably the great mosque in the heart of the city, which originally had been the cathedral church of Saint John but was adapted and rebuilt by the Muslims.

The end of the Ummayyad Empire marked the end also of the single political entity for all Muslims. It was succeeded by a dynasty established in the new city of Baghdad by the Abbasids and by other states in North Africa and the western Mediterra-nean. In time many Muslim states came to exist, but the ideal of a single one, under a caliph (successor) to Muhammad, per-sisted. For several hundred years during which no one power, local or external, was able to dominate the area for more than a brief period, Syria itself became a field on which other Muslim powers struggled for control. Two of the three traditional regional centers of power endeavored to extend and keep their sway over it. Typically, the successive Muslim dynasties that governed from Cairo dominated the southern part of geographic Syria, while Abbasids or semi-independent offshoots from Iraq extended influence over northern Syria. This contest between the Tigris-Euphrates Valley and the Nile Valley has persisted to modern times. The Syrians themselves, under local dynasties in one or another of the great cities, strove to govern themselves whenever possible, taking advantage of weaknesses that appeared in either of the great riverine powers.

LATER INVASIONS

At about the time that the Vikings were colonizing Greenland, early in the eleventh century, the first of a series of movements of nomadic peoples out of central Asia into the Middle East took place. The Seljuks, a Turkish tribe already converted to Islam, swept across Iran and Mesopotamia, taking much of Asia Minor from the Byzantines and seizing Syria. Their interference with Western European pilgrims led to the Crusades, a series of invasions and conquests of the east Mediterranean littoral by armies from Europe. In the long sweep of Syrian history these were fairly minor events, incidents in the centuries of war for control of the region. Politically and militarily, the Crusaders' successes were limited; the Crusader states were confined to the coastal areas and never included Damascus or Aleppo.

But the Christian effort to retake part of the domain of Islam has had consequences lasting to the present day. The French, in particular, thought of France's mandate over Syria in the 1920s and 1930s as redressing the expulsion of the Crusaders. This view and the actions it inspired have not been lost on the Syrians. At the third Islamic Conference Summit Meeting, in January 1981, President Asad of Syria recalled that when the French occupied Damascus in 1920, "The first thing he (the French general) did was to go to Saladin's grave only to say: 'Oh Saladin, here we come again.'"[1]

For it was Saladin, a ruler controlling both Egypt and Syria, who drove the Crusaders from Jerusalem; leaders of a successor dynasty expelled them from their last strongholds in 1291. (Limited in numbers, the Crusaders had relied heavily on their engineering skill in fortress building to secure the countryside. The greatest of their castles are still to be seen in Syria.) But some decades before the end of the Crusader presence, another and far more powerful force had swept into the area. Mongol hordes out of central Asia, under Hulagu, swept across Iran, gave the final blow to the Abbasid state with the sack of Baghdad, moved into Syria, and captured Aleppo. Recurrent waves of Mongol invaders surged into Syria in subsequent years. The last of these, under Tamerlane, inflicted damage in 1401 from which Syria never completely recovered. His armies took and sacked Damascus and lesser cities, as well as Aleppo. Large numbers of artisans and craftsmen were transported fifteen hundred miles (twenty-four hundred kilometers) to the Mongol capital of Samarkand in Central Asia.

What is remarkable is how much Tamerlane found to destroy and to take away. Despite the contention and fighting by outsiders and locals for domination of Syria, over several centuries before the Mongols came, trade, crafts, and intellectual life had continued to flourish. The great caravan routes along the Red Sea to Damascus and from the east up the Tigris-Euphrates Valley to Aleppo and Antioch made those cities wealthy. Though the cities were prizes for invaders, they prospered in the intervals between wars. But being an appendage rather than an integral element of one of the great states of the area took its toll in vitality. When massive destruction took place, the damage proved permanent.

Not that Syria became a desert – its cities remained important and trade revived after the Mongol destruction. When a new power, that of the Ottoman Turks, arose to the north in Asia Minor, Syria was viewed as a prize worth taking. The Ottomans had established themselves in Asia Minor as successors to the Seljuks and, after a substantial setback at the hands of Tamerlane, expanded at the expense of the Byzantine empire, which they extinguished with the capture of Constantinople in 1453. Sixty years later, Ottoman armies took Syria from an enfeebled Egypt – and subjugated the latter country a year later.

The citadel of Aleppo, reminder of Syria's tumultuous past.

SYRIA UNDER THE OTTOMAN EMPIRE

For the next four centuries Syria remained part of the Otto-man Empire, a state far more powerful in the sixteenth and early seventeenth centuries than any of the European monar-chies. Its people were governed by officials responsible to Istan-bul (formerly Constantinople), and for a time they prospered. But eventually Ottoman rule lost its efficiency. By the late eigh-teenth century, misrule rather than competent governance was the norm, tax gathering had become extortionate, and order typically did not extend far beyond the cities. The annual caravan from Damascus for Muslims on the pilgrimage to Mecca—a major responsibility of the governor of Damas-cus—had to purchase protection from the nomad tribesmen along the route. Non-Muslim minorities, which will be dis-cussed in detail later, turned to coreligionists in Europe for protection.

As it had been so often in previous centuries, Syria was

split up according to the needs of powers external to it – in this case the centralized Ottoman state. The Ottomans divided Syria into provinces, one centered on Aleppo, another centered on Damascus, and a province (sometimes two) in the coastal area centered on either Sidon or Beirut. The Damascus province included Jerusalem and surrounding areas until late in the nineteenth century, when Jerusalem received separate status. In the mid-nineteenth century, communal disturbances resulting in heavy loss of life among Christians in Lebanon led Istanbul, under heavy European pressure, to establish a special administration for the Christian area there. This autonomous *sanjak* of Mount Lebanon, supervised but not governed by the European powers, provided the basis for the creation of a separate state of Lebanon by France when it was awarded the League of Nations mandate for the area in 1922.

Even during the Ottoman period, Cairo rather than Istanbul ruled Syria for a time. In the aftermath of Napoleon's invasion of and defeat in Egypt (1798–1801), an Ottoman officer, Muhammad Ali, made himself master of Egypt. Though nominally subordinate to Istanbul, he was in fact independent. In 1832 his armies occupied Syria; the Egyptians stayed for eight years until domestic opposition and military pressure from European states forced them to withdraw. The Europeans were not at that time ready to dismember the Ottoman state and allow its constituent Middle Eastern provinces to seek their own paths. They came to that policy piecemeal a few decades later, beginning with the creation of the *sanjak* of Mount Lebanon in 1864, British de facto rule of Egypt after 1882, and Italian conquest of Libya in 1911. The final dismemberment came with World War I when British forces, in long and heavy fighting, took the Iraqi provinces and, with Arab help, drove the Turks from Palestine and Syria.

Syria's separation from the Ottoman Empire in October 1918 was accomplished by British arms, assisted in no small measure by Arab forces. By 1915 large numbers of Arabs were willing to take up arms against the Ottoman sultan, the nominal political and religious leader of these Muslims. This rebellion came about because of developments reaching back into the previous century. Perhaps the most important of these was the spread of literacy and education, which brought new ideas—many from Europe—to larger numbers of people. Arabs in Syria and elsewhere, attracted by ideas of constitutionalism, supported movements led by Young Turks aimed at liberalizing the political institutions of the empire, specifically the restoration of the short-lived constitution of 1876. In the same period, there developed stirrings in the Arab provinces for autonomy and for a measure of self-government. But when the Young Turks of the Committee of Union and Progress replaced the sultan's rule in 1912, it did not take long for Arabs to realize that the Committee did not envisage giving up Turkey's Arab provinces. This realization encouraged the work of political societies dedicated to Arab political goals; two appeared before the onset of World War I, one of which was centered in Damascus. The age of Arab nationalism had begun, and Damascus was to be at the heart of it.

3

The Environment

TOPOGRAPHY AND CLIMATE

Syria's landscape has undergone little change in the several thousand years of the nation's recorded history. To be sure, people have overexploited the land, particularly through deforestation. Additionally, there is tenuous evidence pointing to a climatic shift a millenium or two ago that allowed the desert to increase at the expense of area suited for cultivation. But the mountains that trap the rain-bearing clouds, the fertile land, the oases, the desert, and the natural routes for human movement are present today as they were when the alphabet was invented or the Kingdom of Ebla was dealing with Babylonia and Egypt.

The eastern coast of the Mediterranean, the land along the southern slopes of the Taurus Mountains (in what is now Turkey), and the Tigris-Euphrates Valley down to the Persian Gulf form an arc. Popularly known as the Fertile Crescent, this swath of land, nurtured in the west and north by rainfall and to the southeast increasingly by water drawn from the two great rivers, has been farmed since before the dawn of recorded history. Over the same centuries, it has provided a route for trade and an avenue for armies bent on conquest. The western end of the crescent was known to the ancients as Syria, a term that until less than a century ago included the land from the Gulf of Iskanderun down into Palestine.

Geographic Syria has long been able to support a sizable population because of a range of mountains paralleling the coast from Turkey until it peters out in the wastes of the Negev Desert. Like the west coast mountains of the United States, they catch moisture-laden air moving over open water, in this case northeastward across the Mediterranean. This rainfall amounts to more than forty inches (one meter) annually at higher elevations in the coastal range, lessens at lower altitudes, and dwindles to steppe conditions of five to ten inches (thirteen to twenty-five centimeters) a year in Syria's northeast. Rainfall amounts to less than five inches in the desert due east of Damascus, a triangular-shaped region that stretches some five hundred miles (eight hundred kilometers) east before reaching the Euphrates. To the southeast the desert extends for more than a thousand miles (sixteen hundred kilometers) deep into Saudi Arabia.

Rainfall is, without any qualification, the most important element in Syria's climate. Where there is sufficient water, crops are grown; where water becomes scarce, there begins the domain of the nomad. Even a great city like Damascus lives indirectly on rainfall, for the oasis in which it was planted and that provides much of its food is watered from streams that originate in the mountains to the west, between the city and the coast.

The line between desert and farmland in Syria is not a fixed one. It shifts from year to year with the vagaries of rainfall and as a consequence of human activities. A strong administration is able to build and maintain the water catchment and irrigation systems that push the frontiers of cultivation into the marginal lands of the steppe. A weak administration cannot protect farmers from the encroachment of the nomads.

Most of the rainfall in Syria occurs within a few tens of miles of the Mediterranean. The bulk of the population lives within seventy-five miles (one hundred and twenty kilometers) of the sea. The coastal plain, which is narrow and broken by mountain spurs reaching the sea, has long supported farming and fishing communities and has a few small ports. The mountains, traditional refuge of oppressed minorities, are well populated; terracing is employed extensively to squeeze as much cultivable land out of the terrain as possible. East of the mountains in the northern half of Syria, plains cultivation is fairly widespread, especially in the area around Aleppo. The larger part of Syria to the east, however, is thinly populated, with its inhabitants for the most part living in villages strung out along the Euphrates and the two tributaries that join it in Syria, the Khabur and Balikh rivers. Considerable growth in agriculture through an increase in irrigated land in the years after World War II brought substantial additions to population in the area east of the Euphrates. What was once the poorest, most remote district in Syria now boasts two provinces connected to the port of Latakia by railroad.

At the end of World War I, Syria was overwhelmingly rural and agricultural. (This statement applies to geographic Syria, but, unless otherwise stated, from here on "Syria" means the modern republic, not the larger geographic Syria.) An unlettered peasantry lived in some four thousand villages, tilling the soil around them. During the nineteenth century, most of these village lands came into the hands of absentee landlords, some of whom owned several villages. The landlords' take typically amounted to 50 percent of the crop. Much of the landlords' share went into the commercial market, either to feed the population of the cities or to be sold abroad in years of good rainfall and subsequent surplus. But the amount of grain that could be moved was limited by the need to carry it on pack animals or in rude carts. There were exceptions to the pattern of landlords owning entire villages – independent farmers could be found in all the provinces. The Druzes especially, a minority living in the south near the Jordanian border, were individual proprietors. Most villages were isolated, roads being poor or nonexistent.

Self-sufficiency for the village and for the country as a whole was critical in that era before mechanized transport had appeared, so the emphasis was on staple crops such as wheat and barley. Threshing was done in the time-honored fashion, by oxen pulling a sledge on the threshing floor. Vegetables, both those suitable for storage and those to be used immediately, were also raised, the latter especially in the districts close to the cities and major towns. For most people, the margin between having enough to eat and being hungry was perilously thin. In average years, Syria could feed itself, but if rainfall was deficient, some did not have enough. The nationwide fluctuations in cereal output were enormous. Good statistics from the Ottoman period are not available, but the following figures from this century illustrate the point: in 1934 Syrian (and Lebanese) wheat production was 327,000 metric tons; in 1938 it was 667,000 metric tons. That rainfall continues to be a critical determinant of agricultural production is shown by an output of 600,000 metric tons of grain in 1973 and 1,600,000 in 1974 in Syria.

PATTERNS OF SETTLEMENT

Patterns of rural life had long been constant. Most of the peoples who inhabited Syria around 1900 had been there for centuries and had developed ways of dealing with their physical environment. In the northern Syrian plain where wood is scarce, a common village mud-brick dwelling was conical in shape; it shed winter rain and gave coolness in the summer. Mountain dwellers commonly built houses of stone, roofing them with poplar logs overlaid with matting and pressed earth. Life was hard and tedious; most villagers were born, lived, and died without ever going more than a few miles from home. They shared these conditions of rural life with millions of other peasants throughout the Middle East.

The desert, of course, was the domain of the bedouin, nomads who wandered with their flocks of sheep and herds of camels in grazing circuits established by custom and by a show of strength superior to those of other tribes. These circuits knew no government-defined boundaries, and the tribespeople frequently were all but free of government control. Although they pressed from time to time on the fringes of the settled areas, the bedouin's overall impact on the life of the country was quite small.

It was (and is) the cities that dominated Syrian society, that were the centers of intellectual and political life, and that, in their role as trading centers, were a great source of wealth. The two largest, Damascus and Aleppo, each counted some two hundred thousand inhabitants at the end of the Ottoman period. Damascus lies in a fertile and well-watered oasis, the largest such oasis on the old spice route that ran along the eastern coast of the Red Sea from Yemen to the northeastern

Mediterranean. It was also the western terminus of a caravan route that ran east through Palmyra to the central Euphrates in Iraq. Aleppo handled the trade between the Mediterranean and the northern districts of Iraq, Mosul in particular. The latter city is closer to the Mediterranean than it is to the Persian Gulf. Aleppo had also the distribution center for the entire northern Syrian plain; its miles of covered bazaars housed the merchants who supplied the goods and the artisans who handcrafted textiles, leather, brass, and other consumer items. Damascus, too, had its artisans. As witness to this fact are the term for a fine fabric, damask, and damascened steel, prized in past centuries for sword blades.

In recent times, the quality of craftsmanship has declined and the type of trade has changed, but the importance of commerce has not altered. Goods for northern Iraq still pass through Aleppo. Transdesert trade is no longer carried in camel caravans. Trucks bring fresh food from the Mediterranean coast, as well as machinery and consumer goods from Europe, to the oil states of the Gulf. As in past times, new commodities or circumstances require changes in patterns of commerce. Oil from Iraq's northern fields has crossed Syria by pipeline since 1935; a large line, opened in the 1950s, allowed Iraqi oil exports to reach about a million barrels a day (fifty million tons a year) by 1960. Tankers load the oil from this line at Banias, which was a sleepy port used only by coastal sailing vessels twenty-five years ago but today is a place of great economic importance to Syria.

In the two great cities and in the smaller ones – Homs and Hama – lived the small group of people who dominated Syrian life. They were the principal landowners, the merchants, and the men of religion and of learning. Under the Ottomans, they traded, ran agricultural holdings, lived well on the whole, and set the tone for the country. Most were Muslims, belonging to the same majority sect in Islam – the Sunni – that the Ottomans did. They were full participants in the Muslim Ottoman state, frequently serving it as civil administrators or military officers, as often as not in other parts of the Empire. Often the members of one family divided business responsibilities, one overseeing the agricultural holdings, another the commercial interests.

THE BEGINNING OF CHANGE

This centuries-old societal pattern lasted almost undisturbed until the beginning of the twentieth century. Then it began to change because of Western commercial interests and the technology that they employed. Damascus was connected to the sea by railroad in 1895; Aleppo, Homs, and Hama were connected in 1906. At about the same time, steel rails joined Damascus to the Muslim holy cities of Mecca and Medina in the Hejaz (today part of Saudi Arabia). In 1914 the railroad from Istanbul reached Aleppo. All these railways were built and/or operated by European, primarily French, concerns. The same was true of the streetcar lines, telephone systems, and electricity plants that followed shortly.

A road system, too, began to supplement the old network of trails suitable only for animal transport, growing most markedly in the period between the world wars. All these developments helped to end Syria's isolation, especially that of its countryside. But one must stress that they were only a beginning. In 1938 Syria possessed 550 miles (880 kilometers) of railroad, part standard and part narrow gauge, in a country of 72,000 square miles (186,500 square kilometers). There was only one motor vehicle for each 625 people in that year.

Industrial development, too, was only beginning at this time. There was not an industrial establishment of any size in Syria in 1914. Goods that were produced came from tiny enterprises employing a few people, using hand tools. In the interwar period, textile factories came to replace a large number of the hand looms previously in use, a few flour mills were constructed, and Damascus saw the start of a small cement factory. These tiny industries, the railways, and the foreign-owned oil pipelines employed a few thousand true "industrial" workers by the start of World War II.

During the same period, educational opportunities became available to an increasing number of Syrians. Enlargement of the school system during the two decades of French control—an average of seventeen primary schools were opened each year—made it possible for some Syrians to get an education in a system different from the traditional religious schools and/or to go beyond primary grades. Those living outside the major cities were given this opportunity by the opening of secondary schools in various provincial capitals.

On the eve of independence, most Syrians lived in an environment not greatly different from that of their great-great-grandfathers. But the possibility of change was in the air, and some beginnings had been made. Certainly, the climate, the terrain, and the rainfall were the same as they had been; but the potential for man-made adaptations and improvements had begun to be recognized. Increasing numbers of Syrians were literate; communications were improving; the possibility of new careers was opening before the newly educated, and not only those from the cities. People had prospects in government, business, and the military of which their fathers could not have conceived.

LIVING CONDITIONS IN MODERN SYRIA

The changes made by humans in the environment have dramatically altered conditions of life for the majority of the population. These changes are manifest in the places people live, the kinds of dwellings they occupy, how they earn a living, what they do for recreation, what they wear, and how they assess what the future holds for them.

Half the population lives in cities that as few as twenty-five years ago bore unmistakable signs of a tumultuous past. Though there were modern buildings, the heart of each of Syria's major cities still lay inside the old defensive walls; a medieval citadel was frequently the most prominent structure. By the 1970s, growth had left the historic parts of these cities in the center of urban sprawl, with the newer parts occupying many times more acreage than the old, congested towns with their covered bazaars, alleys, and ancient caravanserais. A vast amount of new building in the form of multistory apartment blocks, office buildings, and schools fills this acreage. Though extensive, it does not approach American scales of suburban expansion, partly because ownership of private motor vehicles, though growing, is far from universal, and people need access to public transportation.

The sprawling modern city of Damascus.

The growth of the cities has been made possible by improvements in the transportation systems. In a sense, the two feed one another; more and better roads and bus services have provided the means for the people from the countryside to get to the cities. And as more people have come to those cities, the demand for transportation services has grown. The cities themselves offer a variety of attractions for the discontented in addition to the traditional bright lights. Higher education is centered in them, and that is a major gateway to improved social and economic status. The cities provide jobs of many varieties in fields such as construction, trade, and industry. They provide traditional forms of recreation—typically the coffeehouse where men may sit, talk, and pass the time—as well as newer distractions in the form of the cinema and sports. Soccer is played extensively throughout the country.

This pattern of rural people migrating to the cities in search of better paid and less onerous work or, in the case of the unemployed, of any kind of work, is common in many countries, especially less developed ones. In one respect Syria is unique among them, in another merely unusual. It is unique in that not only have first-generation people of rural background migrated to the cities in large numbers, but the leaders among them have led the country for the last decade and a half. The men who have dominated Syria since the mid-1960s, primarily the soldiers but many among the civilians as well, were born in small towns and villages (see Chapter 6). Hence, the dominant element in the cities is composed of people not deeply rooted in city life. Their dominance has caused substantial social, economic, and religious friction with the previously dominant elements.

The unusual aspect also stems from the prominent position assumed by political leaders of rural origin. They have deliberately tried to improve conditions in the provinces, directing development resources to provide services such as schools, electricity, health care, and agricultural aid. The twin purposes of this policy, to make a better life for those in the countryside and to slow migration to the cities, have to a considerable extent been successful. Big and important as Syria's cities are, they are not swollen to the extent found in some other countries — Iraq, for instance, where the capital contains nearly a quarter of the entire population, or Mexico City with its eleven million people.

In striking comparison to the isolated situation of Syria's village dwellers as little as forty or fifty years ago, the condition of the majority of such people by the mid-1970s was much changed. The physical changes are the easiest to describe: access to various social services, vastly improved landholding arrangements, and transportation. But the intangibles have also altered the environment; country dwellers see the world differently and see, simply, more of it than did their grandparents. Through radio and TV they are in touch with affairs outside their villages, and they have an awareness of national and district as well as local issues. They belong to a body politic that is many times larger than the few tens of thousands who composed it at independence.

It is important not to exaggerate the degree of change in the environment. Old ways continue to prevail in many areas; they underlie and modify "modern" accretions. Some developments are not to the liking of everyone in Syria; some changes have resulted in less efficiency or enjoyment than previously existed. Nonetheless, Syrians of the 1970s and 1980s participate to some degree in the technology that has transformed life for much of the world's population over the last seventy-five years. The clothes they wear, the television they watch, and the jobs they aspire to all contribute to the man-made portion of their environment that is continuing to change.

4

The People and Their Culture

Syria is a Muslim society—that is to say, six out of seven Syrians identify themselves as Muslims—and Islam has been the dominant religious, cultural, and political force for sixteen centuries. Under traditional Islam, as practiced by the Ottomans, religion and politics worked together; in fact they were two faces of one reality. Political leaders looked for support to the men of religion (*ulema*) who also provided much of the society's intellectual activity. The *ulema* urged the people to support any Muslim government that could enforce the desirable basic minimum of public order. The Ottomans did that for much of their four centuries of rule in Syria. They were followers of mainstream Islam, the religion professed by over two-thirds of Syria's population. Not surprisingly, the powerful families that dominated Syria until a generation ago were also from that mainstream. Since 1963, however, Syria has been ruled by men professing a secular philosophy of government. This philosophy aims not at eliminating religion but at separating it in most respects from the functions of government. In general, this approach appeals to Muslims outside the mainstream and to many non-Muslims. On the other hand, it lacks appeal for those whose traditional dominance is no longer assured.

SECTARIAN COMMUNITIES

Sectarian differences have played an important role in the modern politics of Syria; hence, a brief discussion of the structure of the population is in order.

Muslim Sects

The vast majority of all Muslims, around 90 percent, are designated Sunni; that is, they follow the sunna, or tradition of Muhammad. A minority accepts the argument put forth at Muhammad's death that his successor as leader of the faithful—not as Messenger, for that role was his alone—should devolve only on his blood relatives. The difference broke into bloodshed upon Muhammad's death; three of the first four successors were murdered. When the fourth, Ali, the Messenger's cousin and son-in-law, was killed, his partisans (Shi'ites in Arabic) supported Ali's son, Husayn, and his descendants. Some Shi'ites believe that the line ended with the seventh successor, others say with the twelfth; the latter are today the overwhelming majority in Iran, include about half the people in Iraq, and are the largest of the dozen religious groups in Lebanon. Other groups split from them over the succeeding centuries. There are some in Syria.

These differences played important parts in the unfolding drama of Syrian history, and for an understanding of contemporary developments some of them need further attention. For several centuries, at least, more than two-thirds of Syria's population has been Sunni Muslim. Sunnis have been the majority in each of the large cities and have formed the bulk of the rural peasant population in all Syria's provinces except Latakia and Suwayda, where Alawis and Druzes, respectively, are predominant. Sunnis were traditionally found in all strata of society, from the powerful city-based "notable" families through city artisans to illiterate peasants and nomads. It was from within the Sunni community that the country's initial political, economic, and social leadership was drawn. By law and custom, under the mandate and in the first years of independence, certain offices were reserved to Muslims. The president had to be a Muslim, and it was inconceivable to Syrians that he, the prime minister, the chief of staff, or many other high officers of state would ever be anything but Sunnis. Those of other sects had their places in a Sunni-dominated society.

Of the non-Sunni Muslims, two groups are conventional

Shi'ite sects. The group that follows the twelfth imam numbers only a few tens of thousands in a rural area of Aleppo province and has no particular political importance or influence. The other, which follows the seventh imam, is named Ismaili for him. At the time of the crusades, this sect – headquartered in Persia – was powerful in central Syria, near Hama. At its most extreme, the sect employed assassination widely as a weapon against its enemies. Killers who were sent forth after extensive use of hashish were called *hashashin* – whence our English word "assassin." Small in numbers today and no longer given to such political action, the sect, together with coreligionists in South Asia, acknowledges the leadership of the Aga Khan; some of its Syrian adherents have been prominent in the political struggles of the past quarter-century.

The two larger minorities – Alawis and Druzes – derive from developments in the Shi'ite branch of Islam in the ninth and succeeding centuries. The origin of the Alawis is obscure. The bulk of them for centuries have lived in the mountain range, Jabal Nusayriyah, that parallels the coast behind the port and coastal plain of Latakia. Alawis account for two-thirds of this area's population; traditionally, the towns were principally Sunni or Christian. Most Alawis worked land owned by absentee Sunni landlords, under extremely onerous crop-sharing arrangements. Whether they moved into this territory after accepting the preaching, and taking the name, of Ibn Nusayr in the eleventh century, or whether they formed a distinct bloc from earlier times, is problematical. Today about one Syrian in eight is an Alawi. Their concentration around Jabal Nusayriyah, however, illustrates the principle that minorities survive best when protected by terrain from the attentions of the majority. The Maronites of neighboring Lebanon, who form a solid block in the Lebanese mountains, and the Druzes of Lebanon and Syria are equally apt examples.

An impoverished people who protected themselves by living in hard-to-reach mountain terrain and by conveying little to outsiders about their religion, Alawis are not widely understood. Their religious belief and practice owes much to Shi'ism; the name "Alawi" indicates a devotion to Muhammad's son-in-law, Ali. Knowledge of their religion is limited among outsiders;

most information ascribes to the Alawis a belief in a divine trinity and the celebration of some Christian feasts. To the extent that a trinity – one that deifies Muhammad and Ali – is part of their belief, Alawis could not be Muslims. The Ottomans treated Alawis as Muslims, and today's Syrian Alawi leaders conduct themselves as Muslims, taking care to observe feasts, to participate in public prayers, and the like. Alawi religious leaders, moreover, have formally proclaimed that they are Shi'ite Muslims and followers of the twelfth imam. The Syrian constitution of 1973 specifies that the president must be a Muslim, and the Alawi Hafiz al-Asad holds the office. Nonetheless, some mainstream Sunni Muslims continue to question whether Alawis have the right to call themselves Muslims.

The Druzes, who account for about 3 percent of the population, similarly are an offshoot of Shia Islam, founded in the eleventh century. Confined in earlier centuries to the Lebanese mountains east and south of Beirut, the larger part of the Druze community has lived in Jabal Druze, a mountainous region near the Syrian-Jordanian border, since migrations in the early 1700s and again a century ago. The Jabal Druze provided the same sort of protection that the Alawis got from their mountains. The Druzes, although practicing a religion that differs in several respects from Islam, are well-enough known and respected by their Muslim neighbors to be accepted as part of the political and religious spectrum. Their reputation as fighters, especially against the French in the 1920s, has no doubt contributed to this acceptance. In this respect they are viewed differently than the Alawis, who, in the eyes of many Syrian Sunni Muslims, were too willing to succumb to French influence in the days of the mandate.

Non-Muslim Sects

Members of non-Muslim minority groups had their status and prospects for life defined by custom and law. The Christian and Jewish minorities were left behind from earlier centuries, the descendants of those who did not convert to Islam. When the Muslims took Syria, its population was primarily Christian and Aramaic-Syriac speaking. The numbers of Muslims who moved in were relatively few, but the attraction of the new and powerful religion changed the religious map of Syria in a few generations to one in which Muslims were the majority. Arabic, of course, accompanied Islam, and over the centuries even the Christians came to speak it as a first language. Today Aramaic survives as a spoken language only in two villages in the mountains northwest of Damascus.

The rugged mountains provided one of the classic sorts of region, beyond easy reach of governments whose troops bore sword, lance, and bow, in which minorities could survive and prosper. The other locale favorable to minorities is the city. There they can offer special talents—those of the linguist, educator, and artisan—in the marketplace and receive protection for the services they render. About a quarter of the people of Damascus and Aleppo, for example, at the time of independence in 1946 belonged to one or another of the Christian sects.

Those Christian groups, ten in number and accounting for about 12 percent of the population, were essentially self-perpetuating. Centuries ago, the lines dividing Christian from Muslim were set, and little crossing of those lines took place thereafter. By changing his religion, the Christian or Muslim would abandon his status in the social structure, becoming "a man without a nation," for his "nation," i.e., religion, gave him his fundamental point of identity in society. In the Ottoman empire, each Christian "nation" and the Jewish one had its head, its chief religious figure. The head represented his sect's interests to the sultan and protected it from overzealous officialdom. There was some movement among Christian groups as individuals or groups were persuaded by missionaries to affiliate with the Roman Catholic church or to become Protestants. And following World War I, several tens of thousands of Armenian Christians who escaped the Turkish massacres settled in Syrian cities and in Beirut.

Educated in larger numbers than the Muslims, thanks to schools run by their coreligionists from the West, Christians served in the bureaucracy and in business. Because of their exposure to Western ideas through education, they were the principal medium through which Western political, social, and economic concepts were first introduced into Syrian life. They participated in politics primarily to represent their sects' interests; as second-class citizens they could do no more.

Nonreligious Factors as Determinants of Status

In addition to sect, a person's identity and position in society depended on gender and family. Traditional Syria was a society in which men dominated; they were merchants, religious leaders, soldiers, farmers, and workers. Women were concerned with home and hearth. Tasks for each, even in agriculture where women did some field labor, were identified by centuries of tradition. Literacy, low in the whole country, was virtually unknown among women. A man's family—and tribal or clan—status and connections marked him as suited for certain roles and unfit for others. Wealth played a part in this system; most political leaders came from monied families. But a "notable" family origin conferred status on a man, even though the family might have fallen on hard times. Entry into the upper reaches of one's community was possible through hard work, luck, or a favorable marriage, and each generation saw new men rise. In these several respects—religion, gender, and family as determinants of status—Syrian society was similar to that of the rest of the Middle East.

TWO GENERATIONS OF CHANGE

In common with the rest of the Third World, Syria has undergone great social changes in the twentieth century, particularly in the two generations from just before World War II to the present. Such influences as foreign control, radio, and, later, television broadcasting expanded educational opportunities, and better transport affected the daily lives of Syrians. The effects were small and limited to a few people at first, but they grew geometrically, influencing ever larger numbers in more and more ways. Change affected individuals differently, with the result that the old and the new often existed side by side. (They still do.) And not always easily, for not every new thing was appreciated by every Syrian. Removal of religious qualifications for certain posts in the state, for example, upset those who had come to believe that their families had, through generations of occupancy, a right to certain offices. City people have not taken kindly to the domination by country folk that has been a feature of Baath rule since the mid-1960s. Nonetheless, in this and dozens of other ways, Syrians are living with change.

Education

In a largely illiterate society, the spread of education has had a massive impact. In 1938, there were a hundred thousand children in primary school, seven thousand in secondary school, and three hundred fifty in the one university, that of Damascus, which had been founded in 1923. In 1976, there were 1.25 million primary students, half a million secondary, and sixty-five thousand young men and women in three universities – Damascus, Aleppo, and Tishrin (the name, which means "October," recalls the October 1973 war with Israel; the university is located in Latakia). A fourth university opened in Homs in 1979. Even these numbers do not mean that every Syrian child is getting an education. Most boys and two-thirds of the girls begin primary school, but large numbers drop out. Nonetheless, literacy is growing, and more and more people find it necessary in an increasingly complex society. It opens doors to political, economic, and cultural opportunities. The professional scribe still plies his trade, writing letters and petitions for the illiterate; many former customers, however, can do the job for themselves or call on their children to help them.

Much of the increase in education has been connected with the cities. Despite great efforts to extend education into the countryside, rural areas in Syria, as in other countries, have poorer schools and a lower pupil-to-population ratio than urban ones. Syria has long been a citified country in the sense that several cities have dominated economic and political life, and it is growing more so. Urban population has risen from about 30 percent of the total in 1940 to over 50 percent today. Given the absolute growth of population from 2.5 million to 9 million in those years, this increase means that over 4 million people live in urban areas – more than a million in Damascus, nearly a million in Aleppo, and close to a million among the three next largest, Homs, Hama, and Latakia. The centers of these cities, with their relics of the past – defensive walls, citadels, and markets – are, as noted earlier, surrounded by those twentieth-century accretions, apartment blocks, government office build-

Lecture at Damascus University; classes are coeducational.

ings, and factories, to provide the necessities of life for the swelling populations.

A measure of change in all this is illustrated by the new status of women. The founding congress of the ruling Baath party in 1947 declared, "The Arab woman enjoys all the rights of citizenship. The party struggles to raise up woman's level. . . ."[2] There were no women at that congress, but in the 1970s women were to be found in significant numbers at party congresses and in the People's Assembly. In half the provinces the top echelon of the party (the branch command; see chapter 6) had a woman serving on it. None has reached the country's leadership circle, although a woman has been minister of culture and national guidance since 1976. There are also substantial numbers of women in the professions, in laboratories and offices, and in the arts in addition to the conventional (even in the Arab world) "women's" field of teaching. As of 1976, ten thousand women had graduated from Syrian universities.

The Family Group

The success of the Baathists in overriding religion, social position, and gender as the factors that determine a person's prospects has been notable. It has been greatest in the case of religion, least perhaps in the case of gender. Being human, the men who lead Syria—not just the president and his immediate circle of associates, but the members of the party commands, cabinet ministers, directors general, People's Assembly delegates, heads of state-run enterprises, and the like—rely on and advance the fortunes of their relatives. This condition is notable in the case of the Asads; the president's relatives have important and powerful positions in the security apparatus; other important military figures also belong to the same Alawi clan that Asad does. Similar, though less significant in terms of the regime's security, family groupings may be found elsewhere in the system. In this sense, the family remains the focus of identity in contemporary Syria.

Indeed, so important is the kinship group and the associated reliance for mutual support on people from the same sect, district, and social level to an understanding of how the country functions that a more detailed description of the president's support group is called for. This description not only explains who the key figures are in the current regime but serves as a model in two respects. First, should President Asad leave office, his successor(s) would create a similar support mechanism out of his own kinfolk. Second, lesser figures in this regime and to some degree almost all Syrians participate in a functioning kinship group; an individual quite often will be a supporter of a more important figure, as President Asad's men are, and will use the power and prestige derived from that relationship to create a relationship with his own supporters that is mutually beneficial.

President Hafiz al-Asad is an Alawi of the Matawirah tribe and comes from Qardahah, a village in the mountain region of Latakia Province. His younger brother, Rifaat, is commander of the Defense Companies, an organization whose sole purpose is to protect the regime. An older brother heads a part of the Defense Companies; a cousin and a pair of nephews have important posts in these organizations. In addition, many of the senior military and security posts are held by Alawis, some from Asad's tribe. Rifaat al-Asad also functions as an adviser to his brother. Beyond these relatives, Asad relies on and gets the support of men who share his social background and ideological outlook.

It is important for today's aspirant to high position in the system to come from a well-connected and Baathist family – important, but not essential, for the party has not been in power long enough to institutionalize such arrangements, and plenty of those on their way up in the system are the first ones in their family to get an education or hold a political position. The first step up the ladder to power and influence is joining the Baath party and, for some, enrolling in the military academy for a career as an officer. It is possible (there are men sitting in the cabinet who prove it) to enjoy considerable status by virtue of professional or technical competence, without belonging to the party. Most such people, however, began their careers before the Baath party came to dominate Syrian political life. Today, and for quite a few years past, the party has presented itself to the young as the way of life. Through the Vanguards program for youngsters, the Revolutionary Youth Organization, and a student organization, the young person cannot avoid learning that the party is omnipresent and that his or her future will be bound up in it.

Communications

The Baath presence is clearly felt in the media, which are state-owned and run by Baath party militants. Of the three national dailies, *al-Baath* is the official party organ. First issued in 1946, it was published or suppressed according to the politics of the moment until the Baath coup of 1963; it has appeared regularly since. Now twelve pages – a bit above average size for a state-supported newspaper not dependent on advertising for operating revenue – it carries international and domestic news, sports, articles advancing or explaining party policies, and considerable coverage of cultural affairs. Of the other two papers, *al-Thawrah* (The Revolution) is the government paper, and *Tishrin* (October) appeared after the October 1973 war with Israel; in recent years it has seemed to reflect the president's views more closely than either of the others. But all three hew closely to the regime's views on all issues. There are, in addition, newspapers in some provincial capitals and publications for organizations such as the trade union federation and the peasants' union. The military establishment publishes a monthly, *Jaysh al-Shaab* (The People's Army), that has a mix of political and entertainment material.

The electronic media are run by the state. Syria's radio broadcasts in Arabic for domestic audiences and also beams transmission abroad. The television system reaches all major and most secondary cities. The Syrian Arab News Agency provides information and commentary drawn from the press and disseminates official statements. All these systems closely follow the government's position and policy. Syria is surrounded by states with radio and television of their own. Israeli and Jordanian broadcasts can readily be picked up in southern Syria. The multitude of stations run by various factions in Lebanon reach most of Syria. Thus, views other than the official one can reach Syrian audiences.

Culture

Writing of a nonjournalistic type has long had a place in Syria's cultural life. With much attention and interest directed at political matters, a number of Syrian authors are noted for their writings in this area. Such, for example, are Abd al-Rahman Kawakibi, who extolled Arab qualities against those of the Turks in the nineteenth century, and Sati al-Husri, whose writings on behalf of pan-Arabism were widely circulated in the period between the world wars. In more literary areas, Ahmad Arna'ut (1892–1948), who wrote several epic novels based on Islamic themes and also translated extensively from Western languages into Arabic, was the principal figure in Syrian literature during the first half of this century. A lively tradition of writing has been continued by Syrians. Some of the more interesting and incisive political work has been written by men temporarily or permanently out of office; Beirut, Lebanon, is a traditional publishing spot for material not acceptable in an Arab author's own country, and Syrians are followers of this tradition.

Under the Baathists, writing is encouraged. Political

material reflects the view of the regime, but fiction, poetry, and drama are by their nature less constrained. The state publishing establishment issues new titles in literature annually, as well as scientific and educational materials. A number of ministries publish specialized journals, for example *al-Ma'rifah* (Knowledge), a monthly concerned with culture and knowledge, and the bulletins of the flourishing archeological department.

In the performing arts, the state also provides encouragement, direction, and funds. Music (both Western and Arabic), drama (much written by Syrians), and professional versions of folk entertainment that combine elements of music and drama are flourishing. The state cinema organization produces several feature films a year. This is a relatively new enterprise and is small in comparison to the long-established Egyptian film industry, which is immensely popular in the Arab world. Syrian films often use patriotic themes from Syria's past, such as the struggle against the French mandatory authorities and the October 1973 war with Israel. The artistic desires of film and stage producers at times conflict with the imperatives of the bureaucracy that supports them; material deemed unhelpful to the government has been produced but not presented to audiences. Painting and sculpture have their place in Syria, centered on Damascus's Fine Arts Union. Subjects vary from traditional patriotic ones to contemporary and experimental productions.

Traditional music has a long history in Syria and the region around it. Music and its accompanying dance are an essential part of many social events, from harvest festivals in the village to upper-class weddings in the city. Singing and instrumental music using lute, winds, and percussion remain popular. Alongside these forms of music, Western modes and instruments are finding a modest home.

The modern and organized cultural life rests on a base of traditional literature and music stretching back over the centuries. It draws on and competes with the older styles, just as contemporary politics and the newer economic structures do. There is thus a certain tension in Syria's cultural life that, though it may take much time, could lead to a phase of creative vigor in literature and the performing and plastic arts.

5

The Formation of the Modern Syrian State

World War I was the catalyst initiating the train of events that brought independence to Syria and to much of the neighboring Arab area. These events also dictated the physical boundaries of the several Arab successor states to the Ottoman Empire and insured that independence would be slow and painful in coming.

Turkey's entry into the war on the side of the Central Powers in November 1914 put hostile Turkish forces in Palestine only a hundred miles (one hundred sixty kilometers) from the Suez Canal, the British empire's lifeline to India. Accordingly, it was in British interests to foment difficulties for the Turks. The sharif (governor), Husayn, of the Muslim holy city of Mecca had long chafed under Turkish rule; prior to the war he had been recognized by many Arabs as a leader not only of Muslims but potentially of the nascent Arab cause. In respect of the Turks his and Britain's aims were congruent: each wanted them out of the Arab provinces. With the aim of achieving the independence of all Arabic-speaking areas east of the Suez he entered into an agreement with Britain. The vehicle for this agreement is known as the Husayn-McMahon correspondence, Sir Henry McMahon being then the British high commissioner in Egypt. It was the first in a series of incompatible undertakings entered into by Britain – later joined by France – for the disposition of the Arab provinces of the Ottoman Empire. Britain excluded from the areas that it was willing to recognize as belonging to a future independent Arab state "Mersin and Alexandretta, and portions of Syria lying to the west of the districts of Damascus, Homs, Hama and Aleppo," i.e., essentially the mountains and the coastal plain. Sharif Husayn did not accept this limitation but agreed to postpone the issue until after the war.

Shortly after the conclusion of this correspondence, Britain and France, in an instrument known as the Sykes-Picot Agreement after its negotiators, divided the Ottoman territories of Syria and Iraq between them as follows: France was to have exclusive control over coastal Syria from the point where today's Lebanese-Israeli boundary reaches the sea up to the head of the Gulf of Alexandretta (today Iskenderun); Britain was to have exclusive control in the southern two-thirds of Iraq. The portions lying between would be occupied by an independent Arab state, or federation of states, but with Britain having special rights in the southern part and France in the northern part – the traditional "spheres of influence." To complicate matters further, Britain's foreign minister Arthur Balfour told the Zionists in 1917 that "His Majesty's Government view with favour the establishment in Palestine of a national home for the Jewish people." The Sykes-Picot Agreement and the Balfour Declaration were communicated to the Imperial Russian Government, the ally of France and Britain. After the Bolsheviks seized power in Russia in 1917, they published these documents, to the dismay of the Arabs.

From the points of view of London and Paris there were good reasons for these several undertakings. Britain believed it imperative not to allow any other power to establish itself in Palestine, so near the Suez Canal. France had long had special interests in the Levant, especially ties to the Catholic communities there. It was determined to extend its influence in the eastern Mediterranean. There was no possibility of harmonizing the desires of those Arabs wanting independence and the wishes of the two European powers when it came to disposing of Ottoman territory. However, by the time they heard of the accords, those fighting the guerrilla war in the desert areas of the western Arabian peninsula and what is today Jordan were committed. They kept on until the Turks were driven out of Syria. Arab forces under Faysal, son of Sharif Husayn, entered Damascus on September 30, 1918, to general rejoicing by the populace. Aleppo was taken at the end of October.

THE MIDDLE EAST UNDER THE ALLIES

With the Turks out of the way, there was plenty of room for the differences in desires and goals of British, French, Arab nationalists, pro-French Syrians and Lebanese, and Zionists to surface. Under the overall military government of the British commanding officer, the coastal areas had a French provisional administration; in Damascus, Homs, Hama, Aleppo, and Transjordan, the provisional government was Arab under Faysal; in Palestine it was British. Efforts at reconciling the claims of the several participants shifted to the peace conference at Versailles early in 1919. Months of wrangling produced no result; Britain and France even wrangled over the interpretation of the Sykes-Picot Agreement; neither was prepared to accede to Arab demands for self-government. Paris supported Lebanese Christian demands for a Lebanon protected by France. U.S. President Woodrow Wilson proposed an international commission of inquiry, which Britain and France refused to join. The solely American King-Crane Commission visited the area, sounded political opinion, and recommended that geographical Syria remain a unit, with a constitutional monarchy under Faysal under the mandatory protection of the United States. (The United States, having been represented in the area primarily by missionaries and educators with no economic or political interests, at that time enjoyed a good reputation among the local population as a disinterested and benevolent power.) Britain was the second choice of the people to hold the mandate. The report was ignored; it represents, however, with reasonable accuracy, the views of the population of geographic Syria, not including Lebanese Christians and Zionists.

As 1919 wore on, France increased its strength in and control over the coastal areas, to the growing apprehension of the Arab government in Damascus. Seeking to stay ahead of British and French moves, Syrian notables gathered in Damascus and in March 1920 asked Faysal to be king of Syria. He accepted. Britain and France objected with vigor; both were approaching the final decisions on carving up the former Ottoman dominions. French forces marched from the coast toward Damascus. At Maysalun, a town near the present Lebanese-Syrian border, they were met by smaller and poorly equipped Arab forces that were easily defeated. The French went on to occupy Damascus. Faysal fled, later to become king of Iraq. The impact of his brief stay in Syria was phenomenal.

> He has never been forgotten in Damascus. Too short for positive achievement, his rule had aroused enthusiasm and loyalty throughout the country. His Government had had more solid foundations in the popular consent than any perhaps since Ummayad times: had it received help it might have endured. The generation which remembered Faisal could never forgive the French, nor give to their rule more than a forced acquiescence.[3]

The mandate was a device developed by the victorious Allied powers to help territories that had belonged to the losers until the populations of those areas were able to stand alone. The mandate for Syria and Lebanon went to France because of its claim of special interests there. That for Palestine, later separated into Palestine west of the Jordan and Transjordan, went to Britain for the same reason. Both were formally approved by the League of Nations in 1922, but the basic decisions had been taken by the Allied powers at the San Remo conference in 1920. The lines followed roughly those of the Sykes-Picot Agreement. By dividing geographic Syria into a zone where British practice and influence would predominate and one where France would control, the Allies ran counter to majority opinion in the area. They also were, in modern guise, continuing a process whereby geographic Syria had been influenced by and responsible to external powers. For the first time since the rise of Islam those powers lay to the west rather than in the immediately surrounding regions.

France deepened the division of geographic Syria into British- and French-dominated regions by further dividing the area entrusted to it under the mandate.

Since the sectarian troubles of the 1860s, one part of present-day Lebanon, predominantly Christian and consisting of the central parts of Mount Lebanon and the adjacent coastal plain but not the port cities of Tripoli, Beirut, Tyre, and Sidon, had enjoyed an autonomous status within the Ottoman Empire, a status that had been required and that was watched over by the European powers. To this part, France, as mandatory power, added in 1922 the four port cities and the rural areas attached to them, plus the Bekaa Valley running north and south behind the coastal mountain range; the additions created a state in which the Christians had a slight majority. This enlarged state, "le Grand Liban," appealed to the Christians, especially Maronites, a group that recognized the Vatican's authority but that used an Eastern liturgy. The Maronites, by virtue of earlier access to education and French patronage, stood to have a powerful position in the larger Lebanon, but incorporation in Lebanon was disliked by most Muslims, Sunnis especially, who looked to Damascus as a logical political focus. Many Syrians also felt that their natural state had been improperly truncated.[4]

SYRIA DURING THE MANDATE

In the area that is the proper subject of this book, France also pursued a policy of political division. Immediately after driving Faysal out of Damascus, the French authorities set up a separate administration for the Alawi area. Under various names, this state of the Alawis was administered separately, save for two short periods, until late in World War II. The French followed the same practices with regard to the Jabal Druze area of southern Syria (now the province of Suwayda). It too was not definitively incorporated into the Syrian state until World War II. Even the heart of Syria was divided into the states of Aleppo and Damascus from 1920 to 1925. These steps were taken for the administrative convenience of France; the two minority areas were markedly different from the bulk of Syria, which was rendered more homogeneous. Some 85 percent of the people of the states of Damascus and Aleppo were Sunni Muslim; most of the rest were Christian.

The moves were unpopular with the vast majority of people in Syria. Among the Alawis and Druzes, opinion was mixed. Some were prepared to accept separate status; others wanted to be part of the larger entity. Two consequences ensued. When the territories were finally united, many Alawis and Druzes were uneasy at losing the benefits of separate French-protected status and at coming under Sunni rule. The Sunni leadership had by that time become suspicious that Alawis and, to a lesser extent, Druzes would be disloyal to Syria.

In one further area, France followed a policy of separate administration, a policy whose denouement was to outrage Syrian opinion. In the aftermath of World War I, Turkey had agreed that a part of the former Ottoman province of Aleppo, the district of Alexandretta, which included the port of that name through which much of Aleppo's trade flowed and which had a mixed population of Arabs and Turks, be included in the French mandated area. Special facilities were arranged for the Turkish element; Turkish was an official language. This system worked well enough until the conclusion in 1936 of a draft treaty between France and Syria designed for the independence of the latter. Concerned that the envisioned change would put Turks under Syrian Arab rather than French control, Turkey pressed France for a larger role in the governance of the district. France, concerned at the trend of affairs in Europe when Hitler was showing his strength, agreed to this condition. Manipulation of the voting rolls gave Turks 60 percent of the vote in 1938, although they were only 40 percent of the population. Change followed; a wholly Turkish administration was installed; and in 1939 the district was formally incorporated into the Republic of Turkey. This change was in contravention of Article 4 of the mandate "that no part of the territory . . . [be] placed under the control of a foreign power." It was judged an outrage by many Syrians, who looked on it as an alienation of Arab soil, but who were powerless to do anything about it. And Arab refugees from the district were an important constituent element in the pan-Arab political developments of the 1940s.

For the heart of Syria the two decades of French mandate were a time of constant struggle on the part of the Syrian nationalists to wrest political power from their foreign overlords. The details are complex and need not be laid out here. Broadly, French efforts to foster a moderate degree of self-rule foundered time and again on the nationalists' insistence that they have real power, not power subject to French "advice." There were some through whom France could rule, but they never constituted anything approaching a majority. And the politician who collaborated too closely with the French lost his standing with other Syrians. This happened, for example, over the 1936 treaty, which was signed but not ratified by the French parliament. In 1938, Syrian negotiators agreed to modifications in favor of France. Their followers in Syria promptly disavowed the changes. The treaty, which had given many Syrians high hopes of independence in 1936, never came into effect. The consequence of the struggle of the nationalists against French rule was a sort of negativism. Those who best represented Syrian attitudes were of necessity in opposition — criticizing, refusing, nay-saying. They got little experience in the constructive aspects of and the administrative responsibilities that go with political power. This lack was to have its effect when these figures of the opposition came to assume office on Syria's independence because the habits of negativism were too deeply engrained in their behavior to be dropped.

The costs of the French mandate are clear: political negativism, Syrian resentment over the creation of an enlarged Lebanon, minority leaning toward France, and majority suspicion of those minorities. But there were benefits as well. French administration established a fair measure of civil order in the country. It made significant additions to the transportation network. It constructed a system of state schools, up to and including the university in Damascus (some beginnings had been made under the Ottomans). The availability of government schools, alongside private ones that either cost money, were religiously based, or both, gave opportunity for education to many, especially in the provinces. A significant number of those who attended the new government secondary schools established in provincial capitals in the 1930s continued their upward mobility by entering the military academy in the years immediately following independence, whence they moved into the political arena.

It took World War II, the fall of France in 1940, and British military presence in the country from the middle of 1941 to set Syria finally on the road to independence. The swift collapse of French military power told the Syrians that their tutelary had feet of clay, and they were consequently disposed to press harder for freedom. Britain, with commitments on many fronts, was prepared to see Vichy France remain in control of Syria. But in early 1941, German aircraft appeared in Syria, and that the British could not tolerate. The next month British and Free French forces invaded and occupied Lebanon and Syria. The Free French leader promised independence to both countries and proclaimed it a few months later. But France was reluctant to leave; its concept of Syrian independence still included a special status for France, which continued to maintain military forces in the Levant. Syrians saw the French as dragging out an occupation and perhaps even trying to restore direct rule. Syrians rioted and protested against the French, who responded by bombarding Damascus in May 1945. Britain stepped in, got French troops back to barracks, and helped to negotiate an agreement for them to withdraw. After a year in which Syria and Lebanon received progressively more international recognition, the last French forces left Syria on May 17, 1946, a day still celebrated with fervor throughout the country.

EXPERIMENT IN INDEPENDENCE

Neither the times nor the qualities of Syria's leaders were appropriate to the beginning of national independence. We have referred above to the habits of opposition and the lack of administrative experience of politicians. These qualities relate to Syria itself, and they were serious defects. But Syrians had long seen themselves as Arabs, Arabs in the political meaning of people who considered the Arab world as rightly a single entity. This belief predated World War I; many Syrians had hoped for the establishment of a single state after the armistice, or at the very least a single state in the Fertile Crescent. The division of the conquered Ottoman provinces into six political entities— Hejaz, Palestine, Transjordan, Lebanon, Syria, and Iraq—or eight if the states of the Alawis and Druzes are included, led to a widespread belief in Arab as well as Syrian circles that the problems of the Arab world were due primarily, if not exclusively, to this division. The corollary of this belief, that unity would solve Arab problems, kept Syrian leaders focused on broader Arab problems, involved Syria in other states' affairs, and attracted other states to involvement in Syrian affairs.

The first external issue arose right next door in an area that had been part of Ottoman Syria and that many Syrians regarded as a portion of their "natural" inheritance. Zionist settlement in British-mandated Palestine had incurred opposition from Arabs. After a temporary slowdown, Jewish immigration to Palestine increased in the 1930s primarily as a result of the anti-Jewish policies of the new Nazi regime in Germany. Arab opposition broke into violence in 1936; it lasted almost to the outbreak of World War II, and Syrians participated on the Arab side. When Jewish immigration resumed after the war and Zionist intentions to create a state became clear, violence resumed. Again Syrians were involved in guerrilla and terrorist activities. In May 1948, the Syrian army joined its Arab neighbors in an attempt to suppress the nascent Israeli state by force. The attempt failed, and Syrian forces did poorly; disappointed expectations caused extensive disturbances in Syria; the people and the army blamed the corruption and incompetence of the political leaders for the failure.

In March 1949, there occurred the first of a long series of events that were to earn Syria the reputation of the most coup-prone state in the Middle East. The army ousted the civilian government and, under its commander, ruled directly. Before the year was out, two more in a series of what was becoming the classic "Syrian coup" — predawn seizure of radio station, prime minister's residence, and army headquarters — occurred. The third coup thrust into power Colonel Adib Shishakli, who dominated the Syrian political scene until 1954. The Syrian military establishment has remained intimately involved in the political life of the country since 1949, sometimes ruling directly, sometimes influencing events, sometimes using a political vehicle.

The political vehicle that in the event became the property of the Syrian military, the Baath party, was the first political party in the Arab world created with the specific goal of achieving pan-Arab unity. It had two separate origins, one among Alawis who fled the district of Alexandretta when it was taken over by the Turks in 1939, the other in a pair of Paris-educated Damascene school teachers, the Christian Michel Aflaq and the Sunni Muslim Salah Bitar. These two gathered followers into the Arab Baath (Resurrection) party under the slogan of "Freedom, Unity, and Socialism." The party began its work during World War II, was formally founded in 1947 with the participation of émigrés from Alexandretta, and played a growing part in Syrian politics from that time on. It was, moreover, founded as a pan-Arab political movement. Arabs from other states participated in it from the beginning, and Baath organizations appeared in Lebanon, Jordan, and Iraq by the early 1950s.

The Baath has consistently portrayed itself as a party of the masses. In fact, however, it has been an elite organization, recruiting among the educated and with its ranks filled until comparatively recent times primarily with civil servants, professional men, educators, and soldiers. Typically, prospective Baathists were attracted to the party while secondary school students. A major vehicle for this recruitment was the string of secondary schools established during the mandate in provincial capitals. Students readily absorbed the pan-Arab doctrines of the party and were attracted also by its doctrines of social betterment. As the fifties progressed, the Baath party came to contain larger and larger percentages of members from the provinces, who harbored a certain resentment at the traditional domination of their areas by the big-city families of wealth and social prestige.

The men who led the political struggle against French domination came almost exclusively from these well-to-do elements of society. They were educated, were the natural leaders, and had experience in international affairs. They were also patriotic Syrians. But their concept of Syria's well-being naturally focused on the interests of their class. They had, with few exceptions, little understanding of the wants and needs of the peasantry and the growing laboring class in the cities. Like similar leaders in other newly independent countries, they were ill prepared to deal with the revolution of rising expectations fueled by increased education and communications.

The signs of potential revolution were there. Protests directed against civilian government for failure in respect to Israel, for example, contained an element of social dissatisfaction. The power of the traditional ruling class, however, is demonstrated by the fact that the only political movement successfully to harness the depressed classes was led by a member of the ruling class. Akram Hawrani, of a Sunni landowning family in Hama, organized peasants there in the Arab Socialist party beginning in 1950. The party was both a vehicle for Hawrani's ambitions for national political power and a genuine effort to reduce the size of the great estates and to distribute land among the peasants who worked it. In a few years it had grown into a powerful force in Hama province.

Hawrani was a contemporary of the Baath leaders. They, too, were committed to social justice for the masses in Syria, although in practice they gave the goal of Arab unity priority. The two sides saw the virtues of joining forces and did so at the end of 1953. The merged Arab Socialist Resurrection party combined the ideological appeal of the Baathists and the substantial grassroots political strength of Hawrani's party. Its strength helped to turn the course of Syrian politics in a new direction in the mid-1950s. The military strong man who had dominated Syria since 1949 was ousted in a coup early in 1954. The coup leaders returned the country to civilian rule, and by staying out of politics for a time, they permitted (in the parliamentary elections of that year) a degree of political choice not known in Syria before or since. The result was a shift to the left, away from the domination of the old families. The merged Baath-Socialist party won a solid bloc of seats; a large number of independent leftists also won; the momentum of success led the left to a dominant position in Syrian politics. Internationally, Syria began to align itself with the newly successful Egyptian President Gamal Abd al-Nasir, to purchase arms from the Soviet Union, and in general to give signs of breaking with the customs of the past.

THE UNITED ARAB REPUBLIC

The twin movement toward the left and toward Egypt started Syria in the direction of a momentous experiment in Arab unity. In these events, the age-old tendency of the Nile and Tigris-Euphrates valley powers to compete for influence in Syria came to the fore. Faced with the rising power of the left, Syria's old political families and their political organizations sought assistance from Iraq, allied with Britain and the United States, and ruled by the descendants of the Faysal who had been ousted from Syria in 1920. The Baath, on the other hand, continued to gain support for the Arab unity that it preached. Especially after Nasir's success in turning the military defeat of the 1956 war to political victory, the Baath began to see him as a leader who could unite the Arabs. And his appeal in Syria and elsewhere in the Arab world among those who wished a change in traditional rulers grew by leaps and bounds in the mid-1950s. He had successfully defied the formerly dominant Western powers.

The Syrian military establishment, though it had permitted the politicians a free hand in the mid-1950s, did not stay out of politics. Moreover, it was divided within itself. Army officers loyal to Akram Hawrani wanted the speedy adoption of socialist reforms; other officers chafed for a chance to live in the presidential palace; a smaller number continued to support traditional political elements; cliques based on geographic origin jostled with one another. Each group contained competing and ambitious elements. By the turn of the year 1957–1958 a majority of the military establishment came to judge that an appeal to Nasir in the name of Arab unity could benefit their various aims. With the enthusiastic support of the Baath and the grudging acquiescence of more traditional politicians, none of whom could publicly oppose the sacred cause of Arab unity, they asked that Egypt and Syria unite. The United Arab Republic (UAR) came into existence on February 27, 1958, and Syria rejoiced.

Expectations of great things that were to flow from this first effort to unite Arab states soon ran into harsh realities. Nasir had been reluctant to take on Syria's problems, and in exchange for agreement to unite he had insisted on arrangements that gave Egypt the dominant position in the union. Primary among these conditions was the dissolution of all political parties; they were in time replaced by an enlarged version of the government-controlled National Union that was the only political organization in Egypt. In practice, due to its far larger population, economic strength, and bureaucracy, Egypt overwhelmed its junior partner. And nature was not kind; the period of the UAR coincided with one of the worst droughts to hit modern Syria. The consequent drop in agricultural production combined with measures designed to socialize the economy brought about extensive economic dislocation.

Within three years, Syrian opinion had turned sharply against Egypt and the UAR. The traditional families that had seen power and wealth drained from them were perhaps the most hostile. The Baath party, which by its preaching of the cause of Arab unity had done so much to create the climate of 1957–1958, had been shattered by the Egyptians' failure to collaborate with it after unity had been set up. Syrians in general had become antagonistic to the Egyptian style of rule, which, however suitable to an Egyptian population for centuries conditioned to centralized direction, ran counter to the political freedom Syria had enjoyed for at least some of the time since independence. Most important, the Syrian officer corps resented being completely subordinate to a command structure that, correctly or not, seemed to the Syrians designed to insure Egyptian control for Egyptian, rather than greater Arab, interests. These feelings were not universal; Nasir had won considerable support among peasants and the working class for his commitment to the "little people," and some Syrians were so committed to unity that they forgave or overlooked any Egyptian excesses.

In time, Nasir overreached himself. Concerned that the Syrian officer in charge of the intelligence and security system, even though a long-time Nasir loyalist, was getting too powerful, he transferred the man to Cairo. Deprived by Nasir's own action of the eyes and ears that had made his control of Syria possible, the union was vulnerable. A group of Syrian officers, acting independently but in harmony with the feelings of a majority, seized control of the government on September 28, 1961. The Egyptians toyed with the idea of resisting, but with only small forces in Syria and no ready means of reinforcing them, Cairo bowed to the inevitable.

The officers who had carried out the coup did not represent any political organization. They stood back while preunion civilians tried to reconstitute a functioning government. With the Baath and the left in extreme disarray, the forces representing the traditional rulers, at the right of the Syrian political spectrum, had a final chance at governing. Elections, although influenced by the military, produced a parliament with many of the same faces as that of 1954. But the momentum that the left had shown at that time was not present, and in its few months of existence the parliament gave general support to the efforts of the government to reverse the land reform decrees of the UAR period and to encourage private enterprise. A series of cabinets, operating without a clear mandate from the country and lacking leadership, succeeded one another. The military establishment, still divided into numerous factions, kept involving itself in political affairs. The officers, being so divided, could show no clear sense of purpose, and the country drifted through the year 1962 with little forward progress.

Early in 1963, a group of senior officers organized a scheme to seize the government. In building their alliance within the military they joined forces with a group of Baathist majors and lieutenant colonels, who turned out to be a far more formidable force than they or anyone else realized. Baathist officers transferred to Egypt during the union for activities that the Egyptians considered inimical to the union had formed a military committee. Irritated at Egyptian domination, these Baathist officers had turned against the party's doctrine of pan-Arabism in favor of concentration on Syria. Stemming from relatively poor rural and small-town backgrounds, they were strong advocates of land reform and other economic changes in favor of the less advantaged sections of the populace. Their leaders were from those very minorities that had had separate administrations under the French mandate, Alawis and Druzes. There were only five Sunnis in the original military committee of fourteen members, compared with five Alawis, two Druzes and two Ismailis. The coup took place on March 8, 1963; by early July the Baathist component had maneuvered their associates out of power, out of the army, and for the most part out of the country. The Baath and, most importantly, its military component have dominated Syria since then.

These developments, coming at the end of two decades of independence, were a crucial turning point in Syria's history. A few sentences will sum up the major changes that the country underwent. With the events of 1963, the center of gravity of

Syrian politics shifted markedly to the left, where it has remained since then; the once-powerful families were in exile, their lands and other wealth taken from them. Only left-of-center political organizations—the Baath, Nasirists, Communists, and some small splinter socialist groups—were permitted to function. Men from minorities hitherto on the fringes of politics came to occupy the highest positions in the land. Enormous increases in the scale of education and of literacy were bringing a marked change to the political culture of the country. Pan-Arabism as a political force in Syria had been destroyed by the failure of the UAR experiment. Verbal homage was still paid to it, but the attention and interest of the men who were behind the scenes in 1963 and came to rule openly a few years later was focused on Syria and its immediate neighbors, Lebanon, Jordan, Palestine (in the form of the Palestine Liberation Organization and its affiliated guerrilla groups), Israel, and Iraq. Not surprisingly, all but Iraq were components of geographic Syria. Finally, the military establishment was deeply, indeed inextricably, immersed in Syrian politics.

6

Political Dynamics

The presidential system under which Syria has been governed since 1971 is the culmination of the developments reviewed in the previous chapter and also of events in the 1963–1970 period. During those eight years, there was continual struggle for power and influence among several groups and individuals. All were Baathist, for the last serious try at power by non-Baathists (a group of pro-Nasirist officers) failed in mid-1963.

It was a weak and divided Baath party that took control of Syria in the spring of 1963. The party had been formally dissolved from the beginning of the UAR period until 1962. Many of its adherents abandoned even informal association with it, disillusioned by the manner in which its leaders had authorized its dissolution without even a pretense of consulting the membership and by the leaders' subsequent inability to achieve any political standing within the UAR vis-à-vis President Nasir. Hence, although the Baath party's still-prominent founders, Michel Aflaq and Salah Bitar, continued to advocate pan-Arabism from their respective positions as party leader and frequent prime minister, they had few followers. Of some five hundred civilian members active in party affairs in the spring of 1963, most had been turned away from pan-Arabism by the UAR experiment and had come to focus their energies and interests on Syria and its immediate environs. This attitude also predominated among Syrians who joined or rejoined the party in the first half of the 1960s. Known as regionalists because of their focus on the Syrian "region," the Baath party's term for an Arab country, a political division within the Arab nation, they challenged the old guard, the traditional party leaders.

The military Baathists as a group had by far the strongest position. They were well organized; they controlled means of force; and they were prepared to use those means. The military committee, for example, acted on its own in participating in the March 8, 1963, coup, ignoring the party leaders' view that the party organization was not strong enough to unseat the government. With one or two exceptions, the military Baathists were regionalists; that and their determination to wield power, plus their rural background, were the common bonds among them. But they differed personally and on a variety of policy issues, as will be seen below.

In the newly reconstituted party, a variety of ideological and personal factions worked to advance their respective causes. One faction, supported by the short-lived Baath regime in Baghdad, which held power from February to November 1963, succeeded at the Baath national (pan-Arab) congress of that year in getting a heavily Marxist program for social and economic affairs adopted as party policy. Others strongly pushed those parts of the Baath platform that called for social justice, abolition of religious qualification for public office, and improvement of rural conditions. This approach was particularly marked among the Military Committee; twelve of its fourteen founders came from poor families, mostly rural. The party's founders and their few supporters remained in control of the Baath's National Command and used it as their power base in attempting to set the pace in Syria.

Not all of the aims of these groups were incompatible. Moreover, the several factions needed one another; none was strong enough to do without support. From the spring of 1963 until the regionalists emerged victors in February 1966, a confusing power struggle went on, with alliances shifting among the contenders. The struggle pitted members of the Military Committee against one another, Alawi against Alawi, longtime Baath militant against old comrade. The instability in the country may be measured by the ten changes of cabinet and/or revolutionary command/presidential council that occurred during the period. The first casualty of the struggle was the Marxist faction, which—deprived of support by the collapse of the Baath regime in Iraq—lost its influential position in mid-1964.

The old guard improved its position marginally in the course of 1965, due primarily to support from non-Syrian Baathists; it could not contend successfully with the regionalists. Already numerically preponderant, they were able, through control of lower party echelons, to control recruitment and so to add to their strength.

In December 1965 the old guard forced the dispute between the regionalists and themselves beyond the point of compromise by dismissing, as party regulations permitted, the party command for Syria. The regionalists replied in February 1966 by seizing power in a violent coup that drove the party's founders into exile and split the pan-Arab Baath party into two, one centered on Syria and one on Iraq, a division that has since had strong implications for Syria's foreign affairs (see Chapter 8).

Unchallenged military dominance of Syria dates from this seizure of power. But the military Baathists were far from unanimous about the proper course of Syrian affairs. Three areas of contention are particularly important. A group headed by the Alawi officer Salah Jadid, joined by the civilians who dominated Syrian cabinets from 1966–1970, was ideologically committed to a collectivist, state-run economy and to support of a national liberation struggle by Palestinians. The forward policy of this faction helped cause the 1967 war with Israel. Continuing this policy after the Syrian defeat, Syria aided Palestinian guerrillas even to the extent of sending Syrian military forces into Jordan in 1970 when King Husayn began his campaign to crush the growing political power of the Palestinians in Jordan and to reestablish his government's writ over all its territory. Hafiz al-Asad and his associates represented within the government of those years a more pragmatic and less ideological approach to Syria's problems.

Personal ambition and sectarian factionalism, in addition to difference in ideology, led to continued infighting even after the old guard had been dismissed in 1966. The fate of the Baath Military Committee members illustrates the extent of this infighting. One of its founders had joined the old guard and left with it. Another, a Druze officer whose troops had borne the brunt of the fighting in the February 1966 coup, mounted an armed movement in protest against lack of recognition of his role. Defeated, he was exiled to Jordan, where he plotted against the regime. Four others were forced out of the army that year. Two more were pensioned off after a disastrous showing by their troops in the 1967 war. Several others were ousted in 1969. The two main factions of Salah Jadid and Hafiz al-Asad, each founding members of the Military Committee, continued their competition, with the former controlling most of the upper organs of the Baath party and the latter concentrating on placing his adherents among the military in sensitive command positions and in critical intelligence posts. The two managed to compromise their differences enough to prevent open dispute for several years.

Asad's move to the top of the Syrian pyramid of power graphically demonstrated the reality of military predominance of the party. At a Syrian regional congress of the party in October 1970, Asad was heavily outvoted by Jadid's adherents, who, controlling the senior party posts, had seen to it that their people dominated the congress. Some reports say that Asad was even barred from entering the hall. He, seeing no alternative or compromise, surrounded the meeting place with armed units loyal to him, dismissed the newly elected Regional Command, and appointed a provisional command of his own. Several months later, the delegates to a party congress, chosen by a party apparatus under his men's control, affirmed his action. He was then the sole survivor, in political terms, of the Military Committee formed during the UAR, having risen from a major in the air force in 1963 to president of Syria.

The changeover in 1970 was bloodless. Although in form a coup d'etat, it could as well be called a change of administration. In a single-party state where those in power succumb to the temptation to "guide" elections to party bodies, it is very difficult, if not impossible, for those desiring a change in either personnel or policies to effect such change by working within the system. Hence, a show of force commended itself to Asad as a means to power. Should an opposition to him develop someday, it would use a similar maneuver, for he has enforced the same type of control over the party apparatus to bar opponents from rising within it.

THE SYSTEM OF RULE

Over the dozen years since he launched his "corrective" movement – its justification was to correct the deviations from orthodox party policy made by Jadid and his associates – Asad has created a system in which he is the undisputed boss. In so doing he has followed normal Middle Eastern practice: in most of the states for most of the time since the end of World War II, one man has been in charge, be he king, military officer, or political strong man. But even the most powerful leader needs mechanisms through which to govern, and these have a certain life of their own in most cases, assuredly in Syria. The section below discusses the main components of the contemporary Syrian state: the Baath party, the military establishment, and the governmental structure.

The Party Apparatus

The Baath party in Syria is a far cry from the few hundred people active in that organization when their military colleagues took over the state in 1963. It is a large organization, with a membership of around one hundred fifty thousand, which directs the work of and is supported by people's organizations for most occupations or interest groups. Through its educational, cultural, and informational activities it affects the flow of information and interpretation of events that reach the public. Leading party members occupy important posts in the bureaucracy. It is regime policy to keep party membership relatively small and to associate much of the population with the system through the people's organizations.

Nominally, the senior body in the party is the National Command, whose status dates from the days before the party split in 1966. This twenty-one-man body, composed of about half Syrians and half Arabs from other states, chiefly Lebanon, Jordan, Palestine, and Iraq, maintains the fiction that the party is serious about pan-Arabism. Syria continues to assert its adherence to the pan-Arab slogans of the past, the slogans that were the driving force of the party's Arab policy in the 1940s and 1950s. But these are not reflected in action. Little effort has been expended in establishing or supporting party formations in countries other than the four neighbors noted above. Asad heads this command, and it provides places for several comrades whose usefulness in domestic Syrian politics has ended.

The twenty-one-man Regional Command, also headed by Asad, directs Baath activities in Syria. Six of its members, including Secretary General Asad, are military officers; two hold the key security posts of minister of defense and minister of interior. Five other command members hold posts in the cabinet of January 1980. Each of the civilian members not holding a cabinet post heads a party bureau or has additional party responsibilities. There are bureaus for youth, students, labor, training, peasants, party organization, and the like. In many cases this responsibility includes supervision of one of the people's organizations.

Subordinate to the Regional Command are a layer of branch commands: one in each of the thirteen provinces; one in each separately administered city, i.e., Damascus and Aleppo; and one in each of the three universities, located in Damascus, Aleppo, and Latakia. Typically, senior members of the local bureaucracy (e.g., the provincial governor, the chief of police) are members of the branch command. But they rarely, if ever, are named secretary; that position, and many of the branch command slots, are held by full-time party functionaries. Farther down the organizational chart, each district of a province, or quarter of a city, has a party organization commensurate with its size; here, too, local administrators are likely to be found on the command. Below the district, the party reaches into subdistricts and villages.

The various commands are the executive organs of the party. The Regional Command is selected at a congress of delegates from party delegates throughout Syria. Normal practice is for a new regional congress to meet every four years, although special circumstances can cause it to be called into extraordinary session. These congresses afford the regime's leaders an opportunity to hear what persons down the organizational chain are concerned about. The seventh Regional Congress, meeting at the turn of the year 1979–1980, was notable for extensive ventilation of the seven hundred and fifty delegates' concerns about the country and the party. Criticism of

corruption and of inadequacies on the part of regime functionaries was extensive and included even President Asad's brother
Rifaat as a target. Half the Regional Command chosen was new;
President Asad and three others are the only ones whose service
on the command goes back to the start of his time in power.

The military forces have a party organization separate from
the civilian one. The two join only at the regional level where,
as noted above, military men sit on the command and where
delegates from party organizations in military units attend
regional congresses. The military side of the party has branches,
enough to provide one for each army division and major components such as missile forces, the air force, and the special
security Defense Companies (see below). The little that is
available on or can be extrapolated from the activities of the officer corps makes it seem that party membership, while not
essential for an officer, is certainly helpful for his advancement
and close to essential if he aspires to flag rank. Save at the top,
there is no civilian-military mixing in party affairs, except for
special arrangements where armed forces personnel provide
paramilitary instruction to members of youth organizations or
to the members of the party militia, the people's army.

Attached to the party, in many cases created by it, are a
panoply of people's organizations. Though the membership of
these is not exclusively, or even primarily, Baathist, their
leaderships are. A partial list includes the Revolutionary Youth
Organization, the Union of Students, the Women's Organization, the Peasants' Federation, and the General Federation of
Trade Unions. Each is under the supervision of a Regional Command member, and a people's organization with a large membership in a given province may have a provincial branch command member responsible for its activities and well-being
there. These organizations serve the purposes of inculcating
Baath values in their members, of organizing the energies of
many segments of society, of providing new recruits, and of
extending services to various components of society. The
Women's Organization provides instruction in domestic arts,
runs adult literacy programs, and encourages the acceptance of
women in roles long reserved for men by tradition. Women
hold positions on several branch commands but have not

attained a post on the Regional Command. A woman has been minister of culture for the past half-dozen years.

The coming generation gets careful attention from the party. In the Baathist state, indoctrination begins early through membership in the Vanguards, an organization for boys and girls in grade school. The principal activity of this group is a summer camp program run by party militants. At later ages come the youth organization and the student union or an occupational organization. Befitting a party founded by teachers, and which for many years recruited its members primarily in the secondary schools and the colleges, the Baath in Syria still emphasizes the educated and the intellectual. The equating of party branches in each of the universities, where student bodies average twenty-five thousand, with branches for provinces with populations of several hundred thousand testifies to that emphasis. Nonetheless, the party has been working consciously for years to increase the ratio of workers and peasants in its ranks.

The party thinks of and describes itself as a revolutionary organization, and in terms of the changes it has wrought in Syria, this is a fair description. But it is also a large bureaucracy, with the reports, paperwork, and offices that a bureaucracy spawns. Members advance, not only by performing the functions required of them, but by progressing through a training program. There is a system of party schools at the various organization levels that run courses for cadres, potential leaders, of varying lengths. The apex of the system is the Higher Political Institute, which is the graduate department of political science at Damascus University, occupying a facility separate from the main university campus.

Governmental Structure

The system of government is highly centralized, concentrating power in the president. The permanent constitution of 1973 institutionalizes changes in the governance of Syria since the coup of 1966 and especially since Asad took power in November 1970. The primacy of the presidential office runs all through the document. Under the constitution the president determines and executes government policy, appoints and dismisses prime ministers and cabinets, promulgates laws, is supreme commander of the armed forces, can veto legislation (the veto may be overridden by a two-thirds vote of the People's Assembly, a right that has not yet been exercised), and has a strong voice in the judicial process. The Regional Command of the Baath party nominates a person to run for the presidency.

The cabinet, responsible to the president, is an executive rather than a policymaking body. Its size has varied, but in recent years it has had about three dozen members. Some cabinet officers, such as the foreign and defense ministers, are close associates of President Asad and have been in office since he took power. Others are technicians. About a quarter of cabinet posts are held by non-Baathists, including members of minor parties associated with the Baath in a national front (see below). Prime ministers and interior ministers have averaged several years in office. The former have been changed when the president has wanted to signal a change of policy to the populace.

Since 1973, Syria has had a people's assembly of members chosen by universal suffrage. Candidates need not be Baath party members, and about a third of those winning election are from outside the party. In sharp contrast to the electoral system in effect until 1961, under which seats were distributed on the basis of religion, the Syrian constitution requires that at least half the assembly's members must be workers and peasants. The assembly has the power to propose laws, to discuss cabinet programs, and to approve the budget. It serves primarily, however, as a forum for discussion of issues and as one of the many conduits through which the government can inform the citizens about its plans and policies and can learn what is important to those citizens. As a component of a highly centralized state, it does not have independent power.

The thirteen provinces plus the separately administered cities of Damascus and Aleppo into which Syria is divided are subordinate in all respects to the central government in Damascus. Provincial governors are appointed with the approval—or by the personal choice—of the president. They report to the minister of interior who, as in most countries of the world but not as in the United States, is responsible for the national police and internal security functions as well as for local administration. Other central government ministries, for example, agriculture, electricity, and transportation, have provincial offices and functions as appropriate. The governors are frequently men of considerable standing in the party; a number have served on the Regional Command, and the current prime minister came to that job from the post of governor of Damascus. Each governor has the assistance of a local council, three-fourths elected.

The provinces vary in size, from Damascus with some nine hundred thousand people to Suwayda with only one hundred fifty thousand. (Qunaytirah has but a few tens of thousands, but much of it is under Israeli occupation, and many former inhabitants live elsewhere in Syria.) Most provinces are centered around a city that has been historically the economic focus of the area; Damascus and Aleppo, Homs and Hama on the route between them, Latakia, and Dayr al-Zur are the most prominent. Each province is divided into a number of districts according to its size, and these have an administrative structure similar to the provinces—a senior official, an advisory council, police, and other government services. Once substantially cut off from the major streams of social and economic activity, the provinces have, under the rule of men born in them, become focal points of government activity in the form of new roads, water projects, rural electrification, and schools over the past decade and a half.

The Military and Security Services

In addition to the civilian government structure and the Baath party apparatus, there is a third element of the governmental triad. This element is less obvious in some respects than the other two; it certainly does not bulk large in a textbook description of the bureaucratic process. But the Syrian regime's single most important source of strength is its monopoly of armed force in the form of its conventional military establishment, security services, and police. Regular military units are usually not used directly in security roles, nor in a political one since Asad took office in 1970. The security services are extremely active in their mission of spotting persons who are sufficiently dissatisfied with the regime to work against it. A certain amount of grumbling is tolerated, as long as the grumblers don't organize. In addition to them and the police who perform the normal functions involved in maintaining civil order, there is a security unit commanded by President Asad's brother, Rifaat. Estimated to contain between twelve and twenty-five thousand men, the Defense Companies are believed to be heavily Alawi in composition and are a mainstay of the regime.

It would be hard to overstate the role of the armed forces in Syrian life. They have been the ladder to the top of the political pyramid for some and a road to superior social and economic status for many. Conscription provides a steady flow of manpower and exposes almost all Syrians to military influence. Only a small number can afford the fee prescribed by law to buy immunity from service, as that fee, once small enough that most middle-class youth could avoid service, has been raised in the course of the past ten years to several thousand dollars. Conscripts serve in an army of two hundred thousand men, well equipped with modern weapons and extensively mechanized. The equipment is entirely from the USSR and has become more sophisticated as the years have passed. Main combat units are deployed on the Israeli front, and since 1976, at any given time about twenty thousand troops have been on duty in Lebanon; rotation has meant that many units have seen service there. Conscription of males provides a common experience for young men, and the government takes full advantage of its opportunity to indoctrinate them with patriotic sentiments and Baath ideology.

It is the officer corps, however, that continues to be the key military element in the political dynamics of Syria. Unlike the situation in this country, cadets in the military academy have long been politicized. Asad and his associates, for example, joined the Baath party while they were in secondary school. So did many others. Through the 1950s, the corps of cadets and the officer corps they entered had men representing various political and ideological schools. The history of Syria up to 1963 is mirrored in the struggles among various factions in the officer corps. After 1963, the Baath created an "ideological army," that is, an army devoted to the Baath party and its goals. Since that time, only Baathists have been allowed to conduct political activity in the armed forces. Baathism became the only political philosophy to which the military were exposed. The armed forces were to defend not only the country but its political system.

In the early years of the Syrian republic, up to at least the middle 1950s, the officer corps roughly represented the ethnic breakdown in the country. With the growth in the armed forces, from forty thousand in 1958 to eighty thousand in 1967 and two hundred twenty-five thousand today, and the increasing availability of secondary education, the ethnic and social composition began to shift. A military career offered opportunities for social advancement to poor boys from the countryside. All the available evidence indicates that in the armed forces, as in the Baath party and the regime generally, men from the provinces predominate. And of these provincials, Alawis are substantially overrepresented in the military as compared to their proportion in the population at large.

Military officers, primarily of provincial and in many cases of Alawi background, have provided Asad with many of his key subordinates over the past dozen years. These are in addition to those from his kinship group (see Chapter 4). Thus, the same man, Mustafa Talas, has been minister of defense and deputy commander of the armed forces since 1971. Critical military posts, such as divisional commands, have been entrusted to loyal subordinates. The post of minister of interior has been held by a succession of officers, most of them Alawi. Other senior officers have been entrusted with important ministries, important provinces, or tricky foreign problems. The prime ministership has twice been held by a general; other prime ministers have owed their rise to Asad's patronage. In what appears to be an attempt to placate sectarian feelings, all have been Sunni Muslims. Some of these subordinates have remained in the circle of loyal and trusted associates for years; others have been retired as scapegoats or as genuine failures.

THE SYSTEM AT WORK

This is the structure within which Asad has worked for the past twelve years. Part of it was in place when he seized power in 1970; part he built himself. In the 1966–1970 period, power had been diffused among a number of senior Baath party figures who came in time to be arrayed in two broad groups, that around Salah Jadid and that around Asad. After ousting his rivals, Asad by steps gathered the formal as well as the actual reins of power in his hands. To a considerable extent the system of governance in Syria today has been designed to President Asad's specifications for his style of centralized rule.

Consolidation of Power Under Asad

Immediately after dismissing the ruling Baath body in November 1970, Asad appointed a provisional Regional Command; he and Mustafa Talas were the only holdovers. When people loyal to him had gained sufficient control of the party branches and sections, elections for a regional congress were held. Meeting in May 1971, this body gave its approval to his corrective movement and named a permanent Regional Command, changed from the provisional one largely by the addition of new members. Asad became regional secretary general. In mid-year, the National Congress met; it too chose Asad to head the National (pan-Arab) Command it elected. He has been reelected to those posts at succeeding regional and national congresses in 1975 and 1979–1980.

While securing his grip on the party apparatus, Asad moved in the political arena. He headed a cabinet as prime minister and appointed a loyal adherent as temporary chief of state. Asad himself took office as president in mid-March, 1971, after nationwide balloting gave him, the sole candidate, more than 99 percent of the vote. (He was to get a similar percentage when he ran for reelection as the sole candidate in 1978). When a single candidate gains such nearly unanimous approval, it does not mean that all but a handful of citizens actively favor or support him. Such overwhelming results are intended to show the citizens and others abroad that the leader, the sole candidate, is incontestably in charge. In 1971 Asad was in charge of Syria. He dominated the party as secretary general, the government as president, and the army as commander in chief. Just as important, his men were spotted through these three organizations and controlled the security services as well.

Asad's first moves set the tone for the first half of his

administration. Substantially less of an ideologue than the men with whom he had shared power, he took a pragmatic approach to Syria's problems. He encouraged the return of Syrians who had emigrated in large numbers to neighboring states by promising, and delivering, a measure of individual initiative in certain economic fields, particularly the services sector. This move did not change the basic socialist nature of the Syrian economy or allow private enterprise into major industries or utilities, but it did offer smaller-business owners a chance to make a profit. It appealed to the Syrian sense of entrepreneurship and resistance to total government control that continues to be a characteristic of the country. Many Syrians took advantage of the offer, and Syria saw a number of its citizens return from nearby Lebanon, many bringing substantial sums of hard currency with them.

In a broader field, Asad moved to involve growing numbers of citizens in the political administrative process. He established a deliberative body, the People's Assembly. Its initial membership, in February 1971, was entirely appointed. Following adoption of the permanent constitution in 1973, elections to the People's Assembly were held, and it began its session in June 1973. Further broadening the political process, Asad invited parties on the left side of the political spectrum to join the Baath in a National Progressive Front. The Communist party and three small Nasirist and socialist parties participated. There was no question of equality in this front; the Baath clearly had the leading role and an absolute majority on its governing body. It, like the People's Assembly, brought into the governing system some useful people and deflected them from notions of active opposition they may have had. The Communists and two of the other groups have been represented in the cabinet since 1972. No part of the right was involved; destroyed by the revolutionary events of the UAR experiment and its aftermath, right-of-center political movements of consequence did not exist in Syria by the mid-1960s.

Successes scored in the October 1973 war with Israel added to the soundness of Asad's position. Even though Syrian forces were unable to capitalize on the success of their initial thrust into the Golan Heights and were driven back beyond the prewar lines, they were judged by Syrians to have performed better than in 1967. In mid-1974, thanks to United States Secretary of State Henry Kissinger's shuttle diplomacy, Syria recovered a portion of the territory it had lost in 1967.

The middle of the 1970s marked the peak of Asad's effectiveness and popularity. The Baathists had been in office long enough to have learned their jobs, yet not so long as to have grown stale. Thanks to Syria's participation in the 1973 war, Arab oil-producing states were providing hard currency payments. The economy was faring well; development program projects were coming into operation; the largest of them, the major irrigation and electricity-generating dam on the Euphrates River, was giving the country a surplus of electricity. Enjoying considerable popularity, the regime was able to keep reliance on its security services mostly behind the scenes. Finally, Syria enjoyed good relations with most Arab states; its influence on its immediate neighbors, Jordan and Lebanon, was quite strong.

Decline in Popularity of the Regime

The foreign factor as an element in Asad's favor has declined since 1976, primarily due to developments in Lebanon. The Lebanese civil war, which started in mid-1975, grew to such proportions that Damascus's very important interests were threatened. Accordingly, Syria dispatched troops to prevent one of the warring parties, the Palestinians, from defeating the other, the Maronites. Up to thirty thousand men were deployed there at the height of the involvement; two-thirds that many are still there. The intervention in Lebanon has been an economic drain and a source of political strain with other Arab states and has brought Syria close to major hostilities with Israel. Although Syrian casualties have been relatively low, opinion in Syria tends to take the line that a long, costly involvement should bring results, not merely a continuation of the same unsatisfactory situation.

Since 1976, Asad's regime has declined in popularity and effectiveness, due much more to domestic factors, both general and specific, than to Lebanon. No single factor is critical, but cumulatively they have put considerable stress on the government. At least one negative element is probably beyond the power of the regime to change, for it is inherent in its structure. The system is cumbersome, very bureaucratic; in effect it has too many people telling other people how, when, and where to do their jobs. In the early years of Baath rule, this cumbersomeness was less of a problem; the bureaucracy was smaller, and many citizens responded favorably to displays of government initiative. But, with time and repetition, what was merely a change the first time becomes a nagging irritation the tenth or twentieth.

The Baath's long tenure has resulted in bureaucratic flabbiness. Asad has tried to ensure that new blood does get to the top. There are, for example, only three members of the current Regional Command whose tenure there has lasted the entire Asad period. Extensive changes have also occurred at party branch levels and in provincial governorships. But certain key figures, including Asad's closest advisers, stay in office, and those who do come up as replacements, whatever their technical, administrative, or other competence, owe their rise to demonstrated loyalty to Asad and his system. None are disposed to take major initiatives. Public complaints about extensive and growing corruption among the ruling elite, including members of Asad's family, surfaced in the mid-1970s and continue to be heard. The extent of dissatisfaction was made evident by the extraordinarily low turnout, less than 10 percent of those registered, at the elections for the People's Assembly in the spring of 1977. Elections held late in 1981 also resulted in a low turnout.

An authoritarian regime that wants to stay in power is constrained in attempts to deal with dissatisfaction by the requirement that it not do injury to those props that are essential to its survival. Asad responded to charges of corruption by inaugurating an anti-corruption campaign in the summer of 1977, with considerable fanfare. It got great publicity for several months and then petered out amid talk in Syria that the misdeeds of Asad's Alawi coreligionists were being ignored, while Sunni Muslims and Christians were singled out for punishment. Talk of Alawi domination of Syria came to be commonplace. Critics of the regime were quick to point out Alawis in key positions or to say, if a key position such as minister of defense or chief of staff were held by a Sunni, that such a person was but a figure-head.

The issue of Alawi dominance of Syria is a key one. It is also a result of the thoroughgoing revolution in Syria that this book has described. The victory of the regionalists in 1966 not only turned Syria away from pan-Arabism, it also marked the end of a revolutionary development that had begun a decade earlier. That revolution destroyed the power of the merchant-landowner, "notable" class based in the big cities. Since the mid-1960s, political, economic, and military power has been held by persons from the provinces who had been completely outside the national power structure twenty years earlier. They were outsiders in two senses: their strata of the population had been subordinate to city families, in the case of Sunnis as well as of Alawis; and within each of the religious and ethnic groups, they superseded the traditional leadership. One cannot find a person who held a cabinet or senior military position in the 1950s – or such a person's son – in a comparable position in the 1980s.

Within that turnover of power, members of one sect, the Alawi, have achieved a position far out of proportion to the sect's size. Paradoxically, the Alawis gained this position by applying Baath principles meant to bring a measure of equality into a society quite rigidly divided into rulers and ruled, haves and have-nots. Under the Ottomans, one's "nation," i.e., religion, determined one's status. Muslims, especially Sunni Muslims, ruled. This centuries-old custom carried on into independent Syria. In the 1940s and 1950s prime ministers and most cabinet ministers were Sunni. Seats in parliament were allocated on a religious basis, roughly in proportion to the share of each religious group in the population. The Baath, influenced by European ideas, worked to abolish distinction by religion and to replace it, in part, with distinction by occupation. There is only one post in Syria today for which there is a religious qualification; the president must be a Muslim. The Baath also espoused economic principles, basically those of social justice, that were directed against the dominant families. These principles appealed to and were adopted by many who were excluded from even aspiring to power by the old system. Not least among those who seized on the nonsectarian and egalitarian philosophy of the Baath were the Alawis of Latakia province, almost all of whose families had for generations worked land for Sunni and Christian landowners under terms that allowed subsistence but little more.

But while the nonsectarian philosophy of the Baath opened doors to minorities, it did not extinguish longstanding cultural attitudes. Especially strong are family relationships, the deeply embedded custom that a man is entitled to rely on his relatives for support and, as a corollary, that he helps his relatives when he is in a position to do so. We call it nepotism, but the term conveys moral censure that Middle Eastern society does not apply. Certainly there is great and growing unhappiness in Syria that Alawis hold many top jobs and that many members of one family are in the government. To a considerable extent, however, such complaints come from the Sunni who lacks a well-placed relative in government and not from the Sunni who holds a good government or party job himself or has an uncle or cousin who does.

What has happened, however, is that one fairly cohesive ruling elite has replaced an older one. Alawis, dominated by members of Asad's own clan and their relatives and clients, have replaced the Sunni "notable" ruling class in the political field. They have done the same to the Sunni officer cliques of Damascus, Hawran, and Dayr al-Zur that dominated the army in pre-UAR days. There are plenty of Sunnis, and Christians too, holding high positions in Asad's regime – for example, the prime minister and the foreign and defense ministers. But such persons represent themselves, not a power bloc. Their status depends on Asad and his support group, of which they are members. And that is a benefit to Asad, a powerful reason that he remains in office. The person whose fortunes are linked to the militarized Baath system, but who thinks Asad may be losing his grip, has no alternative person or group to which he can readily turn.

Likewise, Syrians who never accepted the legitimacy of the Baath regime or who have come to believe that it no longer merits their support lack any means of expressing opposition. The government's rules for comment in the media have permitted citizens to criticize the way in which government policies are carried out, e.g., to call attention to inefficiency or incompetence; but public criticism of policies themselves is forbidden. Some political figures have from time to time printed critical material in Beirut or other foreign places. Internally, save for a very few demonstrations over specific issues—the most notable being riots in 1973 over the draft constitution, which led the regime to specify in the finished document that the president of the republic must be a Muslim—there was little manifestation of discontent until well on into the decade of the seventies.

The Growth of Opposition

Since 1979, the tactics of forces opposed to the regime and the latter's response have shattered the tranquility and stability that Asad's regime had brought to a political arena once legendary for its fractiousness. Assassinations of figures in the regime, mostly Alawis, began in 1976 and continued through late 1978, when they tailed off for a time. Victims included an Iraqi Baathist on the Damascus-based National Command, the president of Damascus University, and the foreign minister (who was only wounded). Syria charged Iraq with responsibility for these and other acts, with good reason. The decline in assassinations and bombings of late 1978 coincided with Iraq's orchestration of Arab opposition to the Camp David Accords and its agreement to pursue a unity program with Syria.

Not all the violence directed at the regime was instigated from abroad, however. There were significant domestic Syrian forces opposed to the regime. Serious troubles began in the spring of 1979, taking the form of attacks on persons, usually Alawis, and government and party installations. These incidents had decided religious overtones; groups affiliated with the Muslim Brotherhood, an organization espousing the restoration of fundamentalist, Sunni Muslim society and government, took credit for many attacks, and the brotherhood was blamed by the government for virtually all of them.

The scale of violence took a sharp leap upward in June when gunmen, with the connivance of a disgruntled army officer, killed some thirty-five cadets at the artillery school in Aleppo. The killing of two Alawi religious leaders in Latakia two months later set off disturbances between Alawis and Sunnis in that city. The regime responded by seeking out and raiding hideouts of the Muslim Brotherhood, arresting whom it could, seizing weapons, and killing a prominent leader. But assassinations and bombings continued. The amount of violence left no question in the minds of Syria's leaders that the terrorists were able to draw on support from a far wider segment of the population than the brotherhood itself.

Asad attempted to deal with the problem in his customary cautious, step-by-step fashion. Immediately following the Baath party's regional congress of December 1979–January 1980, which brought a dozen new faces to the party leadership and to which he promised a larger measure of rule by law, he brought in a new prime minister, reshuffled the cabinet, and replaced senior officials, including provincial security officers. But violence continued; in March merchants in Aleppo and several other cities shut their shops; syndicates of such professionals as lawyers and medical men, supposedly under the control of loyal party militants, called for an end to the state of emergency, in effect for many years, which gave legal cover to the use of special security courts to try suspected dissidents, preventive detention, and the like.

Cumulatively, these acts of opposition were viewed by the regime as very threatening. If it did not respond, opponents would judge it to be weak and would be encouraged to continue their efforts. Asad finally resorted to strong measures. He sent troops from the special security units commanded by the president's brother, backed by regular troops, into the city in March and again in April. They restored order, but at high cost; estimates of the dead ranged from a hundred to nearly a thousand. The regime no doubt did not intend to kill so many, but it certainly acted as if it felt that failure to act would lead to a breakdown of public order affecting the entire country and its own capacity to rule.

The strong action was successful in reducing the amount of violence. But it fell far short of eliminating it. President Asad was the target of a grenade in June 1980; it killed one of his guards. Government forces continued to press dissidents with raids on their hideouts, but government spokesmen admitted to

The older part of Hama on the Orontes River.

over three hundred assassinations of persons connnected with the regime by early 1981. An explosion at the prime minister's office in August 1981 killed a score of people. Frustration on the part of security forces at their inability to stamp out this dissidence has boiled over in incidents of indiscriminate counterterror.

The most serious episode of insurgence broke out in Feburary 1982 when government forces seeking Muslim militants' hideouts in Hama ran into an ambush. The militants, well armed and well fortified in the alleys of the old city, responded to the clash by calling for a general uprising. It took the government forces two weeks to crush the rebels, and they destroyed large parts of Hama's old city in the process. Speakers for the opposition claimed that many thousands were killed. The government has given no figures; it has preferred to publicize support rendered to the regime by those who remained loyal. Significantly, the uprising did not spread to other cities.

The Hama events were the catalyst for the establishment of an opposition front, the National Alliance for the Liberation of Syria. Its members are the Muslim Brotherhood, the Islamic Front, the pro-Iraqi wing of the Baath party, and a number of independent political figures. Its charter asserts that these members have agreed to free Syria from the regime of Hafiz al-Asad and set up a constitutional parliamentary regime. The two religious organizations are the most important; their influence shows in the charter's provision that Islam should be the religion of the country and Islamic law the basis of legislation and reform.[5]

At the start of the 1980s the nature of political discourse in Syria has altered radically. The centralized administration resting on party, army, and bureaucracy continues to function. Ambitious Syrians still try to improve their position and status by working within it. But the regime is under challenge from foes who display both persistence and clandestine skill. Centered on organizations opposing Asad's rule for its Alawi dominance, the opposition includes many who do not share the religious views of these groups but who see them as offering the best means of effectively opposing the government. At issue in the political arena, alongside the question of how well the Baath system will do, is that of whether it will be changed, and, if so, when, by whom, and in what direction. These are topics, affected by economic and foreign policy considerations, that Chapter 9 addresses.

7

A Changing Economy

Syria's economy in 1981 is a far cry from what it was a scant four decades ago. Change has characterized the economy just as much as it has the political structure. Although the alterations wrought in those forty years are not as drastic, say, as those brought about in Russia by the communist revolution or more recently in Saudi Arabia by the massive inflow of oil revenues, Syria's economy can truthfully be said to have gone through revolutionary change.

The country entered independence with some basic economic assets. It was underpopulated. It was basically self-sufficient in food. Its cities held men having extensive mercantile skill and experience. In the western part, basic elements of a transportation infrastructure had been put in place during the mandate. The war had provided a market for grain and for small-scale manufacturing; it brought money into the country, counteracting some of the harm done by the depression. Syria also had the deficiencies of an underdeveloped country (although the term had not come into popular use then). Literacy was low; technically skilled people were few; wealth was concentrated in a few hands; the bulk of the peasantry existed under oppressive land tenure and sharecropping systems; save for textiles, the country manufactured little.

Entrepreneurial skill and ready markets provided by Allied forces during World War II made money for the wealthy city merchants. The bulk of it was made in agriculture, and this sector, in a country without an industrial tradition, attracted further investment. Using machinery made available through the Middle East Supply Center, an organization set up by the United States and United Kingdom to get necessary supplies to

Middle Eastern countries with the least demand on Allied logistics and resources, and war-surplus equipment, Syrians opened up previously untilled land, primarily in the Jazirah, a district north and east of the Euphrates encompassing present-day Hassakah Province and parts of the provinces of Dayr al-Zur and Raqqah. Most of this land was rainfed and used to grow grain. In the valleys of the Euphrates and the Khabur rivers, pumps were employed to irrigate fertile soil for cotton. With a good international market, the latter soon became Syria's principal export crop. By the late 1950s the area under cultivation had about doubled as compared to 1945 – from 5 million acres (2.3 million hectares) to over 11 million acres (5 million hectares). Although some land remained unutilized, most of that readily cultivable was under the plow by the end of the 1950s.

In the political climate prevailing during the early years of Syria's independence, agricultural expansion was carried out by and for the benefit of the well-to-do city merchants. It was, moreover, the driving force behind the economic growth of the period. Partly through the growth of crops, such as cotton and sugar beets, that required processing, it helped to spur an increase in manufacturing during the same years.

But this economic expansion, based to a large extent on the exploitation of peasant labor, took place at a time when some peasants were beginning to agitate against the treatment they customarily received. Political movements opposed, often for political or ideological reasons, to the regime could and did make common cause with the peasants with their essentially economic grievances against the same people. Thus, a component of the Baath party, chiefly from Latakia, inserted mild socialist, social justice clauses into the pan-Arabist, liberation doctrine of its city intellectual founders. And the successful Arab Socialist party of Akram Hawrani, which merged with the Baath in 1953, was composed of peasants from the Hama area who followed Hawrani because he worked to better their conditions.

By the end of the 1950s, economic time was running out for the old regime. The UAR experiment, which was a major factor in destroying the power of the ruling class and in turning

Syria from pan-Arabism (see Chapter 8), proved to be the economic turning point as well. During the union the first steps were taken toward converting Syria from a laissez faire economy to a state-dominated, socialist one. The very wealthy landholding element was on the defensive in an anti-privilege climate and lost its dominant position. Consonant with the independent streak in the Syrian makeup, the forces favoring a moderate form of socialism won out. Syria today limits private ownership rather than eliminates it. At the beginning of the 1980s about two-fifths of the gross domestic product (GDP) remained in private hands.

AGRICULTURE

In numbers of people employed, agriculture is the largest sector in the economy. It provided about 40 percent of GDP in 1953 and about 20 percent in 1977, dropping to about 17 percent in 1980. But the sector accounted for 50 percent of the work force in the mid-1970s and around 40 percent today. Half the population is rural, and though the ratio between urban and rural dwellers has been shifting in favor of the former, the numbers mean that over 4 million people live outside the provincial capitals in small towns and villages. There they make their living off the land directly or by providing services to those who do. And although much remains to be done, the contrast between the 1950s and the 1980s is striking. In addition to changes in land tenure, most villages have schools; year by year more villages are connected to the national electricity grid and to towns by all-weather roads.

The first major step toward freeing the agricultural sector from the pattern of absentee landlord exploiting sharecropper peasant came during the UAR period. This pattern had been criticized by the political forces, especially the Baath party, that had promoted the union. Shortly after its revolution in 1952, Egypt had instituted a land reform program. As with many aspects of life during the UAR, the land reform in Syria followed Egyptian practice more closely than was called for by conditions. In particular it did not distinguish among types of land — some rainfed land was truly fertile, some merely

marginal. The law, issued in 1959, limited a single owner's holdings to 200 acres (80 hectares) of irrigated and 750 acres (300
hectares) of rainfed land. Up to 50 percent more in each
category could be added if the owner had a sufficient number of
relatives. Land in excess of these quantities was expropriated
and marked for redistribution. It turned out that three thousand
persons owned one-third of the cultivated land. The reform
took from them about half of it.

The notion of land reform, putting farmers on their own
land, is appealingly simple. Carrying it out is a lengthy and complex task. The government had to establish which land to take,
devise mechanisms to get it into peasant hands, and arrange to
provide the services – seed, tools, fertilizer – that the landlords
had provided. Expropriation of some 3.7 million acres (1.5
million hectares) took place fairly quickly. But only a few tens
of thousands had been distributed when Syria seceded from the
UAR in September 1961. Further progress was interrupted
by the return to power of political groups representing the
merchant-landowner element in Syria. After the Baath seized
power in 1963 it reinstituted the land reform program and re-
vised the limit on holdings to between 37 and 125 acres (15 and
50 hectares) of irrigated and 200 and 750 acres (80 and 300 hectares) of rainfed land, depending on its location, quality, and
productivity.

During the last half of the 1960s, Baath ideologues were in
control of domestic economic policy. In the countryside their
approach was to concentrate on the establishment of state farms
and cooperative societies as agricultural production units. The
latter gave peasants usufruct rights to land but not ownership.
The cooperatives provided seed, fertilizer, and machinery, but
they also imposed restrictions on crops to be planted, marketing, and purchases of material. About two thousand cooperatives were in existence by 1970. Not all were production units;
some farmers found these associations beneficial in terms of
getting needed services. All in all, however, the system of state
farms and enforced cooperatives was unpopular among the
farming population. Moreover, it did not improve agricultural
output; with allowance for the vagaries of weather, production
in the late 1960s was lower than in the 1962–1963 period.

Agriculture old and new. (*above*) Traditional pastoral scene. (*below*) Modern irrigation in northern Syria; old-style beehive dwelling in the background.

When Asad took command, there were changes in economic practice, although official policy remained unaltered. In agriculture, as in other sectors, pragmatism ruled. The regime opted for better performance at the expense of ideological purity. Many state farms were converted to cooperatives, and the state farm as a significant agricultural factor virtually ceased to exist; there were fewer than ten in 1978. Naturally, there has been argument within the country as to the proper direction of the agricultural sector. The argument focuses on whether cooperatives should grow or shrink, i.e., whether they should be converted into agricultural production units, or their role should be confined to providing seed, fertilizer, marketing assistance, and the like; or whether they should be allowed to decrease further. Through the 1970s, the advocates of the latter view have had the upper hand. Pragmatism, not ideology, has been the guiding principle of the country's agronomists.

The Euphrates Dam

The course of the Euphrates Dam project illustrates the debate. The regime originally intended that the 1.58 million acres (640,000 hectares) to be irrigated by water from this dam would be exploited by state farms. The first areas put into production (in 1978) were state farms. In the past two years, however, there have been strong indications that peasant owners, grouped in cooperatives, will have the major role as succeeding areas of land are brought into cultivation. The reclamation will be a very long process, both for its magnitude and its cost. It will require, for example, 13,000 miles (21,000 kilometers) of main and secondary canals. Costs for reclaiming land are now estimated at $10,000 per hectare. The original target for completion by the turn of the century certainly will not be met. A number of foreign contractors are working various parts of the project and over 123,000 acres (50,000 hectares) are in cultivation. Syria will probably find that a reclamation rate in the neighborhood of 24,700 to 37,000 acres (10,000 to 15,000 hectares) a year is a practical limit. Such a pace will enable the country to avoid costly mistakes.

However fast or slow the Euphrates Dam project goes, if the people in Syria who work the land have their way, the agricultural sector will remain the bastion of private ownership that it is today. Four-fifths of the cultivated land is privately owned or worked by those who lease it from the government, one-fifth is under cooperative societies where peasants have usufruct rights, and only 1 or 2 percent is in state farms. The latter, in the past ten years, have turned progressively into centers for experimentation and demonstration. The state's role in agriculture is most prominent in the choice of crops to grow, in setting prices for produce, and in marketing. The organization of Syrian agriculture, especially the large role for private ownership, reflects an independent streak in the national temperament. Though many farmers had been oppressed by landlords under the old system, they had from time to time rebelled. Peasants want their own land, and they have in common even with their former landlords a tradition of not being subject to *government* direction in economic matters.

ECONOMIC PHILOSOPHY

This independent streak has been a major factor in setting the direction of the Syrian economy even under a socialist regime. The people who came to dominate the Baath party in Syria in the post-UAR period held strong ideological convictions not only about political organization (see Chapter 6) and national liberation struggle (see Chapter 8) but also about economic organization. Aided by those of similar persuasion in the Iraqi portion of the then still-united party, they caused it to adopt a collectivist policy program at the party's pan-Arab congress in 1963. This led to large-scale nationalization and, during the remainder of the decade, to a sharply lessened role for private businessmen throughout the economy. The major step that moved Syria from a predominately private to a largely public sector economy came in January 1965. The one hundred eight largest enterprises were nationalized, one-third of them completely. The other two-thirds had 75 to 90 percent of their assets taken over; these were fully nationalized in 1970. The oil industry, then small and struggling, had been nationalized in the early 1960s. (The pipelines from Iraq were taken over in 1972 from the Western-owned Iraq Petroleum Company at the same time that Iraq nationalized that company.) Banks have been under government control since the Baath came to power in 1963. Of the transportation sector, the railroads, airlines, and ports are government-owned; trucking is private; passenger road service is mixed.

Measured in terms of GDP, three-fifths of the Syrian economy is in the public sector. In numbers of people employed, the percentages are reversed. About two-thirds of the labor force works in the private sector, the bulk in the labor-intensive agricultural area. But there is a host of privately owned businesses, mostly very small — some in which the owner and a part-time relative are the entire staff, some that have one or two salaried employees, a small number with more than that. These firms dominate retail trade, trucking, tourism, real estate, and almost all light industry, and they have a substantial role in construction alongside the big public-sector establishments. Even the larger firms among these enterprises are deliberately kept small to avoid nationalization.

The state's influence reaches into all sectors of the economy, through its ownership of major industries, its control of credit, and its planning process. The socialist moves of the mid-1960s — return to vigorous agricultural reform in the fall of 1964 and the nationalizations of January 1965 — broke the economic power of the merchant-landowner class as the coup of March 1963 had broken their political power. Those who dominate the private sector are not the former "notables" in a new guise, but a growing petty and middle bourgeoisie exercising the talent for entrepreneurship that has long been noted in the Syrian character. The bourgeois ranks are swelled by persons who have enriched themselves in the public service and wish to put their new wealth to use.

The drive toward socialism inevitably had negative effects. Difficulties put in the way of private enterprise caused a substantial exodus of people and money. Poor performance in the agricultural sector, due to the upsets of the land reform and collectivization, was made worse by severe drought in 1966 and moderate drought in 1968. Damage incurred during the 1967 war with Israel, plus the need to replace lost military equipment and provide arms for planned expansion in the armed forces, brought additional strains. Most of the regular budget increase after 1967 went to national security. And what had been a modestly favorable or neutral balance of payments turned sharply negative, as imports rose year by year.

Nonetheless, by 1970 the regime's efforts to remake the Syrian economy were beginning to show results. Agriculture's share of GDP had declined to a bit more than 20 percent. Industry's share had risen to almost 20 percent; most manufactured goods were in the categories of processed agricultural products, e.g., tobacco, sugar, textiles, and fairly simple consumer goods. Projects were underway to add to the industrial plant, and these gave a substantial boost to the construction sector. Production from the small oil fields in the northeast part of the country began in 1968, and oil began to challenge cotton as the chief export money-maker early in the 1970s.

Planning

Planning as a tool for economic development was introduced into Syria during the UAR period. The first plan covered the years 1961–1965; three other five-year plans have succeeded it. Using funds allocated in a separate development budget, the planning mechanism has become a major tool for the regime's use in directing the course of future economic activity. The planners aimed at providing a communications infrastructure and at developing industries that would reduce Syria's dependence on imports. Over the fifteen-year span of the first three plans, overall investment typically fell short of goals by about 30 percent, although the country made substantial economic progress. The fourth plan (1976–1980) took this shortfall into account by setting aside the first two years of its plan period as a time to catch up, completing projects in process and holding off on starting new ones. Preliminary figures indicated that targets for investment were not met, and the fifth plan also started by concentrating on the completion of behind-schedule projects.

Each plan has had a different focus. The first was designed to harmonize Syria's development with the Egyptian planning process. The second put strong emphasis on the public sector; the chief of its projects was the Euphrates Dam, started in 1968, which is the largest single project in the country. The third plan continued the emphasis on the dam; the project took a quarter of planned investment. The plan was doing poorly, but it was saved by the jump in oil prices of late 1973 and January 1974 and by the inflow of funds provided by oil-rich states to their fellow Arab countries confronting Israel. Even though Syria scarcely counts as a factor in international oil trade, price hikes were so large as to make a difference in Damascus's balance of payments accounts.

Hafiz al-Asad's ouster of his ideological and personal rivals in the Baath party and government in November 1970 was not particularly caused by differences over economic matters. He, like his rivals, came from the rural small-landholding class that had seen its sons rise to the pinnacles of power in Damascus. He was committed, as they were, to improving the lot of the rural population and to building a modern economy with a large industrial component. He, like they, saw the Baath party and the government and popular organizations it dominated as the proper mechanism for achieving this end. Yet he differed from them in how to achieve these goals, and that difference had its effect on the economy during the 1970s.

Asad has displayed a pragmatic, "will it work" manner of dealing with problems and issues, rather than an "ideology dictates this" approach. This pragmatism has not extended, say, to countenancing a return to laissez faire capitalism; Asad knows how that system has worked in Syria. Within the framework of a state-directed economy that provides a place for private property, Asad has shown himself prepared to grant a larger role to the private sector than did his predecessors. We have seen earlier in this chapter how this attitude has affected the agricultural sector.

The Damascus bazaar, the traditional retail merchants, reacted favorably to his appearance, sensing that better times were ahead. They were right, for Asad quickly let it be known that persons who had fled abroad for lack of economic opportunity were welcome back in the country, welcome especially to bring some capital and set up a business.

Ancient and modern irrigation works. Water wheel at Hama. (*left*) Dam on Euphrates nearing completion. (*below*)

THE ECONOMY OF THE 1970S

The past ten years have been marked by two characteristics. One is a recurrence of the cycle of rapid growth, slowdown, and leveling off that has repeated itself several times since independence. The other is the continued decrease in agriculture's share of GDP and the increase in the share of services and industry. Prior to the 1970s, Syria experienced two major cycles. The post–World War II expansion ran out of steam in the late 1950s; agrarian reform and severe drought made the UAR period (1958–1961) one of virtual stagnation. Recovery in the early 1960s carried the economy forward for several years, only to be set back by the nationalizations of 1965, a decline in agricultural productivity attributable to the upsets caused by drought and reinvigoration of the land reform, and the flight of capital consequent on these events.

Asad's liberalized policy toward private enterprise in certain sectors of the economy, the removal of rigid ideologues from positions of influence, and good weather set Syria on a new path of rapid growth during the first half of the 1970s. There were low spots; 1973 was a poor year agriculturally. But overall growth averaged about 10 percent a year. Major expensive projects in the development program were completed, and they added to the country's economic base. The Euphrates Dam was finished in 1973, and it began contributing to the national electricity grid a year or two later after the water levels rose high enough to turn the turbines. Cement capacity expanded, a welcome feature for the construction sector, and the first element in a steel industry was inaugurated.

From 1977 on a different picture emerges. GDP rose by less than 3 percent from 1976 to 1977. In the two succeeding years economic growth hovered around 4 percent a year, a little better than population growth. Several factors contributed to the change. Agricultural production dropped in 1977, returned to the average prevailing in 1974–1976 in 1978, and has done well in more recent years. External aid, which began to flow to Syria from its oil-rich neighbors in 1974, developed an erratic quality. It dropped in 1976 because some donors objected to

Syrian intervention in Lebanon that year, was restored in 1977, took a quantum jump in 1979 after the Baghdad Summit of late 1978, and dropped off sharply by 1980, again due to political disagreements. Syria continued to try to push forward with projects planned on the assumption of large amounts of aid; the results were added to negative balances of payments and budget deficits. Inflation added to the problems; it has averaged about 10 percent in 1978 and 1979, rising to more than 15 percent in 1980.

Despite these troubles, which in some respects are of the sort that virtually all developing economies have experienced, the course of development that Syria has pursued for twenty years is year by year changing the structure of the economy. The decade of the 1970s saw continued growth of government as a factor in the economy. By 1976 a steady rise in the growth of services, to which government has been a major contributor, had reached the point that services provided more than half of GDP. The services sector is dominated by trade and government, which are gradually eclipsing other elements of the sector.

Industrial Development

Syria's effort to convert itself from a predominantly agricultural country to an urban one offering to its people a variety of nonagricultural ways of earning a livelihood has involved the expansion – indeed, almost the creation – of many areas of the economy. Industry is a sector that scracely existed half a century ago. In 1980 manufacturing and mining provided 20 percent of GDP.

Suitably for a country with a large agricultural base and great further potential, a substantial element in Syrian industrial development has involved the processing of domestic agricultural raw materials. Textiles, once a major handicraft business, are a growth industry in the form of both cloth and manufactured garments. A principal input is domestic cotton. To achieve self-sufficiency in sugar (an extensively used commodity in a society of tea and coffee drinkers) the government has built sugar beet refineries. In a situation illustrative of the problems of orchestrating economic development, agricultural planners have not been able to get sufficient land into beet production, and as late as 1979 Syria still imported sugar. Facilities for producing canned food products, using local produce, include ones for baby food, as well as for vegetables and preserves.

In the heavier industrial areas, products useful for other sectors of the economy are prominent. Output of cement, a commodity needed in construction, from half a dozen plants is 2.5 million metric tons a year, and more plants are being built. The nascent metal industry produces iron rod and other structural materials. Fertilizer plants using both phosphates and petrochemicals as raw materials are in operation in cities near major agricultural areas, e.g., Homs and Dayr al-Zur. And the consumer has not been forgotten in the industrial sector. Plants for making refrigerators, television sets, and telephones are turning out those goods. Many of the components for such manufactures are imported, and some installations are better described as assembly plants than as factories. But they do exist, and the sector provides jobs for nearly 15 percent of the work force.

Oil Production

Most important of the elements in the industrial sector is Syria's oil industry. The northeastern tip of the country reaches into the geologic formation that contains over half the world's proven oil resources. Stretching from the southeastern corner of the Arabian peninsula, where Oman has modest oil resources, through the giant fields of Saudi Arabia, Kuwait, Iran, and Iraq, the oil-producing strata peter out in the Syrian-Turkish border area. Exploration has found five fields in Syria, all small, that have made the country a net exporter of oil throughout the 1970s. (Oil production began in 1968.) Most of the oil itself is heavy, with a higher sulfur content; Syria exports some of this and imports different-quality crude to blend with its own as a high-quality feedstock for its refinery at Homs, which has a capacity of 120,000 barrels per day (b/d), and a similar one at Banias on the coast. In 1980, Syria produced about 175,000 b/d of which about 100,000 b/d were exported. Since relations with Iraq were mended at the turn of 1978–1979, Syria has aimed to import about 60,000 b/d of crude. Interruptions in Iraqi oil shipments due to Iranian air strikes on oil production facilities during the current hostilities caused a drop in the flow, for which Syria compensated by reducing its exports early in 1981. In April 1982, following an agreement with the Khomeini government to exchange Syrian agricultural products for Iranian oil, Syria closed its borders with Iraq and stopped the movement of Iraqi oil into and through the country.

Net self-sufficiency in oil has been a major boon to the Syrian economy. Its consumption of 110,000 b/d (5.2 million metric tons) in 1980 would cost $1.7 billion in foreign exchange at 1980 prices, more than the value of Syria's exports. The situation of self-sufficiency will change in the years ahead. Syria's known reserves will last for twenty-five years at current rates of production. As consumption rises with industrialization, a growing motor vehicle fleet, and a growing population, demand will overtake production. Unless new fields are discovered and brought into production, this will happen in the course of the 1980s. And Syria will be faced with a smaller version of the problem that afflicts so many developing states: how to pay for needed imports of very expensive petroleum.

A second aspect of the oil industry, and one that antedates Syria's own oil-producing era, is related to the transportation sector of Syria's development. The first oil exported from Iraq came from the fields around Kirkuk. It moved by two pipelines, one across Jordan to Haifa in Palestine and the other across Syria to Tripoli in Lebanon. In the 1950s a much larger line that terminated at export facilities on the Syrian coast at Banias was built. The transit fees paid by the owners of the oil have been an important source of income for Syria. But political considerations have caused the line to be shut down on a number of occasions, at substantial cost to Syria's hard-currency earnings. At the 1980 rate of $0.33 a barrel, a flow of 500,000 b/d would yield Syria $60 million a year. The line's nominal capacity is over a million b/d, but deterioration of equipment during periods of nonuse effectively limits throughput to about half a million b/d.

This modern version of the ancient trade from Mesopotamia, used as a money earner for northern Syria, is only one of the transportation links that are a part of Syria's development. Of the others (ports, railroads, and the road system), all contribute to tying the various parts of the state together and serving an increasingly complex economy. The partition of geographic Syria left the Syrian Arab Republic shorn of the seaports it had traditionally used. The transfer of the *sanjak* to Turkey in 1939 put Alexandretta, the normal outlet for Aleppo, in foreign hands. Haifa ended up in Israel in 1948. Beirut, in Lebanon, continued to be used as a major funnel for goods. But Syria wanted its own outlets. Even before the start of formal economic planning, some improvements had been started at Latakia. Now Latakia, in the 1930s usable only by vessels loading offshore, into barges, can service dry-cargo vessels alongside piers and handles over 2.5 million metric tons of cargo annually. In 1965, work began to develop Tartus, then usable only by coastal sailing vessels. Since 1969 the capital of a separate province, it too can handle over 2.5 million metric tons a year. Most of Syria's nonoil trade moves through the two ports.

The port of Latakia has been linked to northeastern Syria by a railroad completed in the mid-1970s with Russian help. The agricultural produce of both the rainfed lands in that area and the land to be irrigated as a result of the Euphrates Dam scheme will be able to move to factories, consumers, and the ports via this line. Plans are drawn to connect Damascus directly to Homs by rail, obviating the need to use the mandate period rail line that runs through Lebanon. From Homs a line already runs north to join with the Latakia line and at Aleppo with the Turkish system, which in turn ties into Iraq's rail net (this is the eastern end of the Berlin-to-Baghdad railway that imperial Germany envisioned in 1900). Total route mileage amounts to 1,035 miles (1,670 kilometers). The other major transportation service owned and operated by the state is Syrian Arab Airlines. Its fleet of fourteen aircraft is chiefly used in external service; it links Damascus with cities in Europe, the Middle East, and Asia from its center at Damascus's international airport. Work is in hand to run some international service through Aleppo. Road transport is the domain of private operators. It carries a substantial share of internal trade and also operates interstate traffic into Jordan and to the oil states of the Gulf.

Trade and Aid

Foreign trade is a major element in the Syrian economy. Over the 1970s, it has grown at a rapid rate. Exports grew rapidly in the period, primarily due to the jump in oil prices at the beginning of 1974; the value of Syria's exports went up by 150 percent from 1973 to 1974. Oil and cotton are the principal items; they and small quantities of other agricultural produce account for nearly 90 percent of exports. Despite the good export performance, the decade saw a rising deficit in the balance of trade as imports increased faster than exports. The deficit was £S 6 billion ($1.5 billion) in 1977. A major factor has been an increased share of imports being devoted to capital goods, material designated for the development program.

For a country having close political relations with the USSR and its COMECON associates, Syria does not trade heavily with them. The share of those countries in Syria's trade dropped steadily from 1969 to the late 1970s. In the import category it has stood at about one-fifth of the whole for several years; exports to Communist countries went down from one-third to a one-fourth over the same period. In 1978 only 20 percent of Syria's total trade was with Communist countries, in 1979 just 17 percent. By 1977, half the trade of Syria was between it and Western Europe. The Arab states account for about one-sixth of the trade. No small part of the COMECON and the West European trade is connected with development projects. France, the Netherlands, West Germany, and Spain are among the contractors involved in activities ranging from harbor dredging and land reclamation to fertilizer and tractor factories. Among the Easterners, the USSR built the Latakia-Qamishli railroad, the Euphrates Dam, and such other enterprises as factories and irrigation works.

External aid has become a vital element in the Syrian economy. It is far and away the major source of capital for development, as well as for military purchases, and to a lesser degree, but still importantly, for consumer goods. The several sources provide aid in very different ways, on vastly different scales, and for different purposes. The largest amount comes from Syria's fellow Arab states. After the October 1973 war with Israel, oil-rich Arab states made continuing payments of financial aid yearly to Syria as a confrontation state. (Egypt and Jordan also received money.) Although dissatisfaction with Syrian moves against the Palestinians in Lebanon during 1976, especially on the part of Iraq and Libya, caused a temporary drop in the flow of this aid, it continued and was raised still higher at the Baghdad Arab Summit Conference of November 1978. Called to organize opposition to the Camp David Accords of September, the meeting struck Egypt from the roll of aid recipients and drastically increased the share of the other two states. The annual subsidy promised to Syria rose to $1.85 billion.

Contributions have remained high, although political differences have caused fluctuations. Syria agreed at the time of the Baghdad conference to work with Iraq with a view to uniting the two countries. Neither was very optimistic, but considerable activity went on over eight months. Then the regime in Baghdad – where Saddam Husayn had just succeeded Ahmad Hasan Bakr in the office of president – announced the discovery of a plot against it, hinting that the plotters were acting on behalf of Syria. The unity talks came to a halt, but Iraqi aid to Syria continued into 1980. Other suppliers have continued to provide financial aid to Syria. Saudi Arabia has held up its contribution at times to underscore its views of what should be appropriate Syrian conduct in inter-Arab affairs, but it has paid the money it agreed to at the Baghdad meeting of 1978. Libya's president Muammar Qaddafi has contributed larger sums than he was actually committed to, possibly as much as $600 million in late 1980 after Syria agreed to unite with his country.

This Arab aid has been intended for Syria's use to bolster its military capabilities vis-à-vis Israel. And budgeted outlays for national security nearly doubled from 1978 to 1979 and remained at the level of £S 8.5 billion the following year. However, the regime in Damascus conceives of national defense in terms more broad than strictly military expenditures. Hence, it uses Arab aid money for projects that will strengthen the economy. Money provided by Arab states under the rubric of confronting Israel has gone into port expansion, highways, and improvements to Damascus airport.

Of Western aid sources, the United States was for a time the largest. Relations between the two countries improved dramatically after the 1973 war, with Henry Kissinger's success in arranging for Syria to regain some of the territory it lost to Israel in 1967. Between 1975 and 1979, $438 million in aid was authorized for Syria, a rate of about $90 million annually. About two-thirds had been used by 1981 when opposition to Syrian policies in Lebanon provoked moves in the Congress to stop aid to Syria; the administration did not propose any aid after 1981. The World Bank has been a significant donor, providing over $400 million in project aid for advances in a variety of fields from irrigation to education. The European states have done little in the aid field bilaterally, only a few tens of millions of dollars annually.

Assistance from COMECON countries is of long standing, beginning on a small scale in 1957. The USSR has provided aid in a variety of areas, the largest – and Syria's largest single project – being the great dam on the Euphrates. The USSR and its associated states have provided technical assistance, loaned money, and generally assisted in many areas of development. The amounts total $1.8 billion over nearly 25 years. One area in which the USSR has been most involved, but about which little can be said with precision, is that of military supply. Over the years since Soviet military equipment began to arrive in Syria, in the 1950s, the USSR has reequipped the Syrian armed forces after heavy losses in 1967 and 1973. It has provided successively more up-to-date and sophisticated weapons. These have amounted to hundreds of aircraft, the latest model being the MIG-25; thousands of tanks; armored personnel carriers; artillery pieces; surface-to-air and air-to-air missiles; and a host of the other equipment that a modern army needs. How much Syria has paid for this, how much it still owes, and over what period its loans extend is not known with certainty. During 1980 it was reported that the USSR had forgiven a quarter of a $2 billion Syrian military debt and that Qaddafi had paid the USSR an additional $1 billion on Syria's behalf.

What is certain is that the requirements of national security have been a heavy burden on the Syrian economy. The fighting in 1973 did an estimated $1.8 billion worth of damage.

Military expenditures continued to grow during the course of the 1970s. By 1977 Syria's armed forces numbered about two hundred twenty-five thousand men, equipped with increasingly sophisticated weaponry. According to official figures, expenditures for national security accounted for three-fifths of the ordinary budget and a quarter of the combined ordinary and development budgets in 1976. Expenditures climbed to over $2 billion in 1979 and 1980, nearly a third of the combined budgets. There is reason to believe that these sums do not represent the totality of Syrian military expenditure, for some defense expenditures, e.g., external procurements, do not appear in the published budget.

The military establishment is a heavy user of manpower; the two hundred twenty-five thousand men serving in them were equivalent to about 12 percent of the labor force in 1975. The armed forces have not grown as rapidly in the last few years, and with population growth this percentage will decline somewhat if the armed services do not expand significantly. The internal security expenditures of the government, budgeted at $100 million in 1980, and the manpower tied up in security functions in four principal intelligence and security organizations are an additional drain. The exact size of these organizations is unknown, but their representatives are ubiquitous.

It is not only the requirements of national and internal security that take people away from productive economic work. In addition to these, the state employs three hundred thousand people. By all accounts, state establishments run to overstaffing and redundancy. Another distraction of personnel from economically productive work is the Baath party bureaucracy and the associated one that staffs the people's organizations. Most party members hold jobs, either civilian or military. But there is a sizable cadre that staffs the various bureaus and offices, the training system, and the upper levels of the mass organizations. The work cadre members do is judged politically necessary by the regime. They provide useful channels of information to and communication from the regime. Many of the most ambitious Baathists are in this professional cadre. Their work is valuable in building a political structure, but their considerable energies are denied to the building of the economy. Conservatively, 5 percent of the labor force appears to be involved in nonproductive work. This, plus a current 10 percent in the armed forces, is a heavy drag on an economy trying to develop and grow.

THE NEXT DECADE

As Syria moves into the 1980s, there are a number of indications that its economy is not in the best of health. Inflation continues to run in double digits. Military expenditures remain high, a condition that is likely to persist as long as involvement in Lebanon, poor relations with neighbors, and above all a state of hostility with Israel dominate Damascus's foreign horizon. And despite their commitment to economic betterment for their people, Syria's leaders are directing most of their attention and energies to the country's internal security problems. As a measure of their distraction, the fifth five-year plan was not issued until August 1981 although ministers had discussed its goals and general levels earlier in the year.

There are long-range problems for the government that will become more pressing in the 1980s. Domestic oil production will be overtaken by demand during the decade, as was mentioned above. Syria will no longer be a net exporter of oil but will have to spend precious foreign exchange on oil imports. Demand for electricity, too, is showing signs of outrunning the country's generating capacity, despite the large quantities produced by the Euphrates Dam. It met 85 percent of the country's needs in 1978 but less than 60 percent in 1980. Planners are considering a nuclear power station and oil-fired ones; either type would be costly. And there are no indications that the weight of large numbers of unproductive people in the military forces, security services, and bureaucracy will be any less in this decade than in the last.

To dwell solely on the Syrian economy's problems would give a misleading picture. Under the rule of the Baathists substantial improvements in the economy have been effected, not only as measured by growth rates, industrial production, and agricultural output, but also judged by the standard of living of the population. People live longer, eat better, and dwell in more comfortable homes than in the recent past. The country has a good transportation infrastructure, growing numbers of literate people, and sufficient arable land. Finally, Syrians have, more often than not, shown an ability to solve problems in ways that favor efficiency (make it work) rather than doctrine (how it should be). This capacity appears, for example, in the government's tacit approval of a substantial shift to a private rather than the ideologically favored collective approach to agriculture.

To sum up, the Syrian economy has undergone great change in the country's short life of independence by any standard of measurement, be it sectoral distribution of economic activity, urbanization, or industrialization. Inevitably, in undertaking and forcing this change, difficulties have arisen, inefficiencies have emerged, and mistakes have been made. For ". . . if a country had the administrative and technological capacity to organize a rapid development and expansion of its economic activities, it would not be an underdeveloped country."[6] There are certain to be further problems. The heavy burden of military expenditure is not likely to be lifted any time soon. Political disturbances will affect the economy. But the economy will not sit still; the forces set in motion will continue to affect affairs. Further change is certain, and continued betterment is likely.

8

External Affairs

Syria's place in the tumultuous world of Arab politics has changed remarkably in the last four decades. For the first half of this period, up to the early 1960s, Damascus was a principal voice of pan-Arab nationalism, a role it had had since World War I. In keeping with this tradition, it was the birthplace of the first Arab political party with unity as its object, the Baath. Baathists preached the doctrine of pan-Arab unity, aided by pan-Arabists not affiliated with a political organization. Their efforts were a major factor in the great rise of pan-Arab sentiment in much of the eastern Arab world—Libya to Iraq—in the 1950s.

Syria itself was an object of the attentions of other Arab countries as they tried severally to achieve positions of dominant influence there. The late King Abdallah of Jordan, fired perhaps by the failure of his brother to rule long as king in Damascus, strove to link the two countries under himself. After his death in 1951, his Hashemite cousins in Iraq worked toward a similar end. With the rise of Gamal Abd al-Nasir in Egypt, the latter country competed with Iraq for influence in Syria, a twentieth-century version of the age-old rivalry between Mesopotamia and Egypt over the area. The title of the best book on the period, *The Struggle for Syria*,[7] precisely characterizes what went on. The outcome of the struggle was the formation of the United Arab Republic (UAR) of Egypt and Syria in 1958. Its failure—Syria seceded in 1961—signaled the end of the phase in which ideas of unity dominated inter-Arab politics.

As regards Syria, the phase of pan-Arabism ended for two reasons; because of political changes in the country and because of attitudinal changes elsewhere in the Arab world. Chapter 6 described how a faction of Baathists called regionalists rose to power. These men have seen the proper priorities for their country as domestic development, affairs in geographic Syria (their immediate neighbors) and Arab world affairs, in that order. As will be discussed below, trying to arrange matters within geographic Syria to even the slight satisfaction of the Baath rulers has frequently required Syria to involve itself intensively with other Arab states. But the involvement has been that of separate entities collaborating with one another, not that of the parts of an Arab nation seeking to unite.

This approach on Syria's part has been possible because most of the Arab world has ceased to be mesmerized by the prospect of Arab unity as a practical political goal. Compared to the 1950s, there is now little popular enthusiasm for the cause of unity. Over the 1960s and 1970s, solidarity and cooperation for specific purposes have replaced overarching slogans of pan-Arabism. There are exceptions to this generalization, of course; Libya's Muammar Qaddafi is a strong advocate of pan-Arabism. But he has had few followers outside his own entourage. Iraq's Baathist regime has put considerable work into founding and developing Baath party units in other Arab countries; it is serious about unity but sees the road to it as taking time and careful preparation. Most Arab states have needed to focus on their own concerns, collaborating with one another as required for specific purposes and by their actions downplaying political unity.

Syria's external concerns are far from inconsequential, and they affect the nation's internal affairs as well. It has been deeply embroiled in the Arab-Israeli issue since before it and Israel came into independent existences. Syrians were extensively involved in providing aid to Arab forces during the 1936–1939 uprising in Palestine; they fought in the wars of 1948–1949, 1967, and 1973. Syria has a longstanding special interest in Lebanon. Its relations with Jordan, to the south, have varied from closeness to bitter enmity, with affairs tending in the latter direction more often than in the former. All three states exist on land that Damascus regards as of special importance to itself. It would like to wield special influence in the area, considering geographic Syria to be what the European nations used to call a sphere of influence. Syria sits athwart important communication lines to northern Iraq; one of the latter's oil export outlets (closed as of April 1982) crosses Syria to the Mediterranean. Until the 1970s it was the only line of major consequence to Iraq. The issue of dealing with Israel has brought Syria into the closest terms with Egypt, when the countries collaborated in a successful surprise attack on Israeli forces in 1973, and has driven it to extreme hostility, following Sadat's trip to Jerusalem and subsequent signing of a peace treaty with Israel.

SYRIA AND ISRAEL

The question of Israel—its existence and how it should be dealt with—has bedeviled Syrians since the 1930s. With other Arab states, Syria in 1948 sent its forces into Palestine in an attempt to prevent the establishment of the state of Israel. These forces took some territory, subsequently made into demilitarized zones, but otherwise were unsuccessful. Their performance, far below expectations, led to charges against political leaders that corruption had resulted in inferior military supplies to the army and was a direct cause of the army's intervention into politics in 1949. From 1949 until the mid-1960s, Syria's mode was the conventional one of refusal to recognize Israel, verbal hostility, incidents along the border, participation in the Arab boycott—in general, taking a negative attitude. Of the three-quarters of a million Palestinians who fled or were driven out of Israel during 1948–1949, about a hundred thousand ended up in Syria. The government, along with those of the rest of the Arab states, did not extend citizenship, for that action would have acknowledged that the Palestinians' right of return to their homeland was in question, but in most other ways it treated them as citizens.

Only with the emergence in power of the Baath in the 1960s did this approach change. Among second generation Baathists the ideas of a national liberation struggle had taken root. These ideological attitudes were particularly strong among the group of Baath regionalists that dominated government policy from 1966 to 1970. In 1966, Syria extended support to a new, struggling guerrilla organization, Fatah (a reverse acronym for *harakat al-tahrir al-filastiniyah* [Palestine Liberation Organization]). This support took the form of money and training and encouragement of guerrillas to conduct operations in Israel by way of Jordanian territory. In 1967, Damascus grew more bellicose; its support for guerrilla activity and especially its charges in May that Israel was massing troops for an attack started the chain of events that led to the Six-Day War the next month. Syria's own military performance was poor; Israel easily captured the Golan Heights, amounting to about half of the province of Qunaytirah. Syria also lost large amounts of military equipment, including much of its air force.

The crushing defeat administered by Israel to the Egyptian, Syrian, and Jordanian armed forces caused convulsions in the Arab world. Palestinians, believing that the confrontation states had shown their incapacity to deal with Israel by normal military means, turned to unconventional, guerrilla activity. Fatah, already in existence, grew rapidly; other guerrilla organizations sprang up. Syria founded its own, Sa'iqah (Thunderbolt), in 1968; headed by Palestinian Baathists, it recruited from Palestinians in Syria and Lebanon. Syria's commitment to liberation struggle separated it from the Arab mainstream. It refused to attend a meeting of Arab heads of state in August 1967 denouncing the resolutions passed by the participants and foregoing financial aid offered to the three states that had lost territory to Israel in June. It castigated Egypt for accepting United Nations Resolution 242 in November, 1967, which called for Israel to withdraw from territories occupied in the recent hostilities. Acceptance of that formulation clearly, if indirectly, acknowledged the existence of Israel, and Syria's leaders at that time were not ready for that step.

During the years immediately following the Six-Day War, support for the Palestinian guerrillas also served Syria's purpose by putting pressure on Jordan's King Husayn. Monarchy was not a favored form of government in the view of Syria's leaders; and Husayn had allowed a group of dissident Baathists to mount a coup attempt from Jordan in 1966. He was forced, by the reputation and the domestic support from his own Palestinian citizens that the Palestinian guerrillas were achieving (as much of it due to publicity as to accomplishment vis-à-vis

Israel), to concede to the guerrillas more and more freedom of action. Much of their support flowed through Syria—where the authorities kept them under close surveillance. By 1970 the guerrillas, or fedayeen, in Jordan had become virtually a state within a state. Husayn recognized that if they were to continue to expand their ability to act without regard to his government's rules, he would personally lose ground to them, and as a result elements of his own regime might turn against him. Hence, he determined to oust the fedayeen from Jordan and initiated military action against them in September. Driven out of Amman and under heavy pressure by Jordanian forces, the fedayeen appealed to Damascus for help. Syria responded by dispatching an armored force, ostensibly of Palestinian Liberation Army troops. A combination of Israeli threats to intervene, vigorous Jordanian military actions, and lack of air cover caused the Syrians to pull these forces back in a few days.

Just what went on in the councils of the Syrian government at the time is still a matter for speculation. That there were differences of view about policy toward the fedayeen and Israel is certain. That the army was still smarting over the beating it took from Israel in 1967 is probable; it would have hesitated before risking a new fight with the Israelis on ground not of its own choosing, and before rearmament and retraining were completed. Whatever went on, the troops went without air support; Hafiz al-Asad was minister of defense; he used the failure of the move as the occasion to take power six weeks later.

With Asad's emergence at the top of the Syrian power structure, a new approach to the Israeli issue quickly became evident. Asad was more pragmatic, far less ideological, than his erstwhile associates. He continued to support the fedayeen, but he worked hard to insure that, to the greatest extent possible, they would serve as an arm of Syrian policy. Not for him was ideological support for several thousand gun-toting young men free to choose to fight or not where and as they wanted. The Palestine Liberation Organization continued to have its headquarters and to hold meetings in Damascus. Guerrillas were armed and trained in camps in Syria. But when it came to operations from Syrian soil, they were under tight control. The consequence was that many of them moved to Lenanon, which, of the four states bordering on Israel, was the one with the least effective government. In time this move would cause grave problems for Asad, but in the early 1970s it was a plus for him.

He continued to build up Syria's military capability. Its army grew to over one hundred thousand by 1973. Asad promptly mended relations with the new president of Egypt, Anwar Sadat (Nasir had died in September 1970 at the height of the Jordanian crisis), joining him, Libya's Muammar Qaddafi, and President Jaafar Numayri of the Sudan in a charter to work for federation. The federation was formed without Sudan, which was distracted by domestic strife, in April 1971. A year later Sadat, Asad, and Qaddafi were sworn in as its tripartite presidential council. Superficially, this looked like a serious attempt at unity, and on Qaddafi's part it was. The Egyptian and Syrian presidents were not serious about creating institutional links among the three states. The federation, however, gave them a means for close collaboration and for planning the military action that they mounted in 1973. Halfway through the three years between seizing power and engaging in war with Israel, Asad made a major change in Syrian policy; he accepted United Nations Resolution 242 of November 1967. Admittedly, he made the acceptance conditional on realization of the rights of the Palestinian people and on Israeli withdrawal from all Arab territory taken in 1967, but these conditions were the standard Arab interpretation of that resolution, which had been skillfully crafted so that the Israelis read it as requiring withdrawal from some (amount unspecified) territory and the Arabs as requiring withdrawal from the all of it.

The course of the October 1973 war is too well known to require elaboration here. Egypt and Syria planned their assaults across the Suez Canal and into the Golan Heights to take place simultaneously. The two Arab forces achieved surprise because neither the Israelis nor any outside observers believed that they were capable of keeping a major attack secret or of executing one effectively. The initial assaults of both countries succeeded in penetrating Israeli defenses. In the Golan, the Israelis recovered and after stiff fighting pushed the Syrians back, taking additional territory, before turning their main attention to Egypt. A cease-fire between Israel and Syria was arranged in late October, but it was frequently broken in the seven months before U.S. Secretary of State Henry Kissinger persuaded the two sides to agree to a separation of forces and convinced the Israelis to withdraw far enough that Syria could reclaim a slice of the territory it had lost in 1967. It reoccupied the town of Qunaytirah June 26, 1974.

Kissinger tried the following year to work out twin second-stage disengagement of forces agreements between Israel and Egypt and Syria simultaneously. Asad refused to go along with the attempt; he felt that his situation differed in essence from that of Egypt. The latter had a wide expanse of territory in the Sinai; there was room for a step-by-step approach. The situation in the Golan Heights was different. There were but a scant dozen miles in the Golan. Israel felt strongly that Syrians should not regain control of the Heights overlooking the Sea of Galilee and the lands north of it. Hence, Israel would not turn back sufficient additional territory to Syria for Asad to consider it worthwhile.

In addition, Syria was much more intimately involved with the Palestinians and their future than was Egypt. A second-stage disengagement on the Golan would not advance a permanent settlement of the Palestinian issue. There were by the mid-1970s some four hundred thousand Palestinians in Lebanon; fedayeen activity from that country had grown enormously. Attacks into Israel from "Fatah-land," an area of southern Lebanon controlled by the guerrillas, went on through the year 1975, and Israel responded with reprisal raids. The situation was one that, from Syria's perspective, could suck it into hostilities on unsuitable terrain almost without warning. Asad therefore held out for the sort of mechanism that Arab leaders had favored for years, a conference that would bring all Arab parties, including the PLO, into discussions, thus maximizing Arab bargaining power. Sadat of course saw it differently; he signed a second-stage disengagement agreement in September 1975 and was promptly attacked by the Syrian media.

In the years since, additional factors have come into play. Israel has established some three dozen settlements with over four thousand inhabitants in the Golan Heights. A movement in Israel aims at annexing the occupied Golan Heights. It won support in the Knesset but failed to pass that body in 1980. In December, 1981, the Israeli government extended its law, jurisdiction, and administration to the Golan. The Begin administration has also put in hand a program, mixing persuasion and mild coercion, to get the Druze inhabitants of the area to take Israeli citizenship. Syria warns them not to; they are in the unenviable position of being pawns.

The mid-1970s, nonetheless, found Syria at the high point of its effectiveness externally. Asad's domestic position was sound. The economy was in good shape, getting infusions of hard currency from the oil-rich states as agreed to at an Arab summit meeting after the 1973 war. The relative military success of 1973 still carried luster. Two of Syria's Arab neighbors were, if not prepared to follow Damascus, at least subject to Syrian influence or pressure. Jordan had mended relations and was collaborating with Syria in a variety of economic and administrative areas. Civil war began in Lebanon in 1975, and Syria felt compelled to intervene militarily in June 1976. This move was carried out expeditiously, and the Saudis arranged a cease-fire and a way for the Syrian troops to remain, under the auspices of a newly created Arab League Deterrent Force toward the end of the year. Iraq, facing a still-powerful shah of Iran to the east, had agreed to Syrian terms for fees on oil moving to the Mediterranean via the Kirkuk-Banias pipeline because it then lacked sufficient alternative oil export facilities. And the Syrians, filling the lake behind the newly completed dam on the Euphrates, were reminding Iraq that the third party downstream on a river system is in a vulnerable position.

Since the mid-1970s, however, Syria's position in the Middle East has deteriorated greatly. Some of that deterioration may be ascribed to internal political difficulties (discussed in Chapter 6), which have lessened Syria's prestige in the eyes of other Arab states. An additional cause is the rise to prominence of Iraq, which under the direction of a newly assertive leadership seized the occasion of Sadat's 1977 trip to Israel to rally Arab states in opposition. But at least as important an external factor in this decline has been the involvement in Lebanon, which has absorbed the energies of Syria's leaders, been a drain on its resources, and tied up substantial military manpower.

THE LEBANESE MORASS

Lebanon has a special place in Syrian hearts. While many could have accepted France's establishing a separate entity for the Christian population of the area, the addition of largely Muslim districts to the Christian heartland to form an enlarged Lebanon immediately after World War I rankled in Damascus and has continued to do so. Although recognizing Lebanon as a separate state, a fellow member of the Arab League, and a participant as an equal in dozens of Arab and larger international organizations, Syria also sees Lebanon as a part of itself, more so than it does the rest of geographic Syria. At most times, Syrians and Lebanese move across their common border with the minimum of formalities. Neither country has ever established an embassy in the other's capital. Syria under a variety of administrations has been prepared to intervene in Lebanese affairs when such intervention seemed to it to be required.

Lebanon's system of government is based on the premises that elected officials represent their religious community and that the higher posts should go to members of the largest communities. The leaders of those communities agreed in 1943 (the National Pact) that the president was to be Maronite Christian, the prime minister Sunni Muslim, the speaker of the parliament Shi'ite Muslim, and the parliament itself was to have a ratio of six Christian seats to five Muslim. The various sectarian communities were led by a small handful of "notable" familes. The system worked for a good many years, but Lebanon changed and the system did not; neither had it any provision for change. The twin bases of the system—a majority of Christians in the population and domination of each community by its traditional rulers—came under heavy challenge from within the country. No census has been taken since 1932, but most observers of Lebanon believe that, due to higher birthrate, Muslims came to outnumber Christians in about 1970 and that Shi'ite Muslims are now the largest single community. Particularly within the Sunni and Shi'ite communities, increased educational opportunities, exposure to political ideas from other Arab states, and desire for opportunity caused people to try to limit the power of the traditional leaders, both the "notables" from their own communities and others of national status. A short, fierce civil war in 1958 was in part a struggle of new forces against the old-time leadership. It was sparked by the Maronite Camille Chamoun's attempt to have himself reelected as president. Syria, then part of the UAR, helped the opposition to make his position untenable.

Lebanon was not in the best of political health when a new catalyst in the form of the Palestinian guerrillas began to move into the country. (Lebanon had been a somewhat unwilling host to a share of the Palestinians who fled the 1948–1949 fighting.) Particularly after being driven out of Jordan in 1970–1971 and rigorously controlled in Syria, the guerrillas turned to Lebanon where they found political allies. The latter were the constituent elements of the National Movement, a coalition of leftist parties and Muslim activists whose goal was a change in the system of government by representatives of religious communities. Each party was glad to use the other, the Palestinians to get freedom of action for operations against Israel, the National Movement to use Palestinian armed might to pressure the establishment to loosen its hold on power. The Maronites and the Muslim establishment, which had relatively little support, were determined to resist; the former appealed to their people's old fears of becoming second-class citizens in a Muslim state. Tensions grew, and in April 1975 full-scale civil war broke out. The army, reft by the same sectarian tensions as the citizenry, dissolved. Within a space of months, the system of government, based on careful balance among the sects, simply collapsed under the strain of events and forces it was not designed to cope with.

Syria watched the developments with increasing concern. Although its basic sympathies were on the side of the National Movement, of which the pro-Syrian Baath party in Lebanon was part, the Movement was showing signs of trying to occupy traditional Maronite territory. The Maronites threatened partition, and the destruction of the state in that fashion would give justification to components of the Syrian body politic to do the same. Moreover, a Maronite state would ally itself with Israel. The Syrians warned in late 1975 that Syria would "reunite" with Lebanon to prevent its partition. A National Movement–Palestinian victory would have spurred partition and would in all likelihood have brought the Israelis into Lebanon in force. They were already supplying and training the Maronite forces.

In early 1976, Syria tried mediation; it arranged a modification of the traditional power-sharing among the communities, which got tentative agreement from many Lebanese leaders but was soon overtaken by military developments. Syria then sent Palestine Liberation Army units from Syria to try to separate warring factions. Nothing worked for long. Finally, in June 1976, Asad ordered the army into Lebanon. It pressed the National Movement–Palestinian forces back, stabilizing Maronite control of that sect's traditional areas. Other Arab states, notably Egypt and Iraq, criticized Syria and sent help to the forces opposing it. By the fall of 1976, the Arab states recognized that Syria was not about to pull out of Lebanon and, through the good offices of the Saudis, arranged a reconciliation among the Arab states and a cease-fire in Lebanon. Syrian forces and some small contingents from other Arab states were constituted as the Arab Deterrent Force in Lebanon.[8]

In the intervening years there has been little progress. Both major protagonists in Lebanon became disenchanted with the Syrian presence. The Syrians themselves, to assure that no one force in Lebanon should become too powerful, ceased defending the Maronite side as it grew in strength. They tilted toward the National Movement–Palestinian side while attempting to keep major fighting from breaking out again. Syria stayed clear of the fighting when Israel invaded and occupied southern Lebanon early in 1978 in an operation designed to damage the Palestinian forces and prevent them from being able to mount raids into Israel. The Israelis withdrew when a United Nations force moved into the area.

In 1981, Syria came close to open warfare with Israel. The latter encouraged Maronite forces to extend their area of control beyond traditional Maronite territory. Syria responded militarily; Israeli aircraft shot down Syrian helicopters; Syria introduced antiaircraft missiles into Lebanon. The last-named two events went beyond the levels of military action to which Syria and Israel had previously limited themselves. It took intensive diplomacy by an American intermediary to get the Maronites out of their forward position and the catalyst of a particularly damaging Israeli raid on Beirut to arrange a broad Israeli-PLO cease-fire. Technically the arrangement was with the government of Lebanon, but that is a diplomatic fiction.

Lebanon remained a shattered land, much of it in the control of private armies. Syrian troops were concentrated in the eastern part and along the highway from Damascus to Beirut. Israel's invasion of June 1982 struck the Palestinian forces in Lebanon a devastating blow. The Syrians also took heavy losses both on the ground and in the air; they were pushed a good distance north, and their antiaircraft missile batteries were destroyed. Israel, occupying Lebanon from Beirut south to its own border, is promoting the establishment of a Lebanese government under strong Maronite domination. Syria has little capacity to help forces friendly to it. Accordingly, Damascus' goal of promoting the establishment of a government in Lebanon that holds views favorable, or at least not harmful in major respects, to Syria's interests is no closer than it was five or six years ago.

As Syria has been seen to be ineffective in promoting its goals in Lebanon, its standing among its fellow Arab states has diminished. Jordan, which collaborated closely in the mid-1970s with Syria, to the point where Palestinian leaders became seriously concerned that the two were approaching agreement on a settlement for the West Bank that they would dictate to the PLO leaders, has turned away from that closeness. Jordan viewed Iraq, which provided growing financial assistance, as a better partner. In a direct affront to Syrian aspirations for leadership in geographic Syria, King Husayn publicly associated himself with Iraq and lent extensive support to the Iraqi war effort against Iran in 1980 and 1981.

INTER-ARAB RELATIONS

An additional factor in Syria's trend toward looser relations with other Arab countries is tied to Egyptian moves. The trend began with a parting of the ways with Egypt over the latter's acceptance of a second-stage disengagement with the Israelis in September 1975. Relations with Iraq had been strained since 1968, when the Iraqi Baathists seized power in Baghdad and gave sanctuary to old-guard Baath leaders ousted from Syria in 1966. Syrian and Iraqi Baathists each considered themselves to be the legitimate successors to the original party. But in the early 1970s the Iraqi regime was on fairly poor terms with almost all the Arab states, and Syria was in company with the majority.

Egypt's move into pariahhood started the events that were to put Syria outside the mainstream of Arab affairs. When Anwar Sadat decided to visit Israel, he told Asad of his plans in advance. The latter was adamantly opposed. He took a leading part in founding the Steadfastness and Confrontation Front — Syria, Libya, the PLO, the People's Democratic Republic of Yemen, and Algeria — to oppose Egypt. Iraq refused to join that front in 1977, but following the Camp David Accords of September 1978 its leaders saw and seized an opportunity to break out of their isolation. They organized a meeting of Arab heads of state in Baghdad, where, through an adroit mixture of modifying their own very hard-line positions on Israel, cajoling, and threatening those refusing to cooperate, they lined up all the Arab states but Oman and Sudan against Egypt.

At the same time, an exchange of messages between Baghdad and Damascus led to a meeting of the Iraqi and Syrian presidents, who agreed to try to resolve their differences and unite. Whatever he may have felt that the chances of success were, Asad agreed to try. The two regimes signed a charter for joint action with the goal of bringing about the closest form of unity possible between Iraq and Syria. Under this charter, joint committees for information and cultural affairs, economic and technical cooperation, military cooperation, and education and scientific research set to work. The days in 1973 and 1974 when Syria refused to let Iraqi oil cross its territory until Baghdad agreed to a stiff transit fee and when Iraq complained bitterly that Syrian filling of the lake behind the new dam on the Euphrates was depriving Iraqi farmers of vital water were, if not forgotten, at least not mentioned. Syrian charges that Iraq had been responsible for assassinations of Syrian officials were also ignored.

There was in fact little likelihood that even a pro forma unity would result from these efforts. To have agreed to even superficial unity would have required either that one Baath party leadership be declared superior to the other, which would have demanded a condescension that neither would make, or that the two parties share at least nominal authority – an impossibility for as independent-minded a pair of leaders as one was likely to find anywhere. The joint committees met with considerable fanfare early in 1979, but momentum had slowed greatly by midyear, when Saddam Husayn, as new Iraqi president, hinted that the Syrians were involved in a plot against him. In my view there almost certainly was no such Syrian involvement, or even a plot; President Husayn brooks no differences from his views, and the fifty-odd "plotters" were, as far as available evidence indicates, guilty of no more than thinking aloud how certain policies, including foreign ones, might be changed.

Whatever the case, activity aimed at achieving unity between the two states came to a halt. Syrian-Iraqi relations reverted to the antagonism that has characterized their association since Baathists took power in 1968. In these circumstances, Syria began to show favor toward the post-shah regime in Iran. Several high political and clerical figures received warm welcomes in Damascus in the winter of 1979–1980. When hostilities broke out between Iraq and Iran in September 1980, Syria did not side with Arab Iraq but with Persian Iran. Its aid to the latter was verbal rather than material, but the policy illustrated how far out of step with the majority of Arab states Syria had gotten.

Once the fortunes of that war turned in Iran's favor, Syria's opposition to Iraq came more into the open. Syria and Iran agreed on a large-scale exchange of Syrian phosphates and food for Iranian oil. With this agreement in hand, Syria closed its borders with Iraq in April 1982, charging Iraq with sending arms to opposition forces inside Syria. Next it shut down the Iraqi oil export pipeline, even though it had used Iraqi oil itself. Promised Iranian oil, Syria took the risk; it also put at hazard the aid money it has been receiving from Gulf states, which were annoyed at Syrian support for Iran.

The majority of Arab states took Iraq's side in its war with Iran, some very strongly. Jordan was the most vigorous supporter. King Husayn was pulled toward Iraq by economic aid and away from Syria by the deteriorating domestic situation there, especially Asad's severe repression of Sunni Muslim fundamentalists who had backers in Jordan. Syria grew increasingly frustrated at its inability to eliminate religious-based opposition forces in the country; it accused Jordan of actively supporting those forces. Finally, angry at Jordan for publicly siding with Iraq, it sought to pressure Jordan by massing troops on the border. It refused to attend an Arab states summit meeting held in Amman in November 1980, which discussed the Iraqi-Iranian war. Joined in this refusal by Algeria, Libya, and the People's Democratic Republic of Yemen, Syria compelled the PLO to boycott the meeting. Thus, in its efforts to create an environment favorable to its interests in geographic Syria, Damascus by 1980 could count on influencing some components of the PLO and few others in the Arab area.

Syria's relatively friendless state goes some way toward explaining its third formal start at creating a union of two or more Arab states since Asad came to power, again with Libya. Without advance public notice, Colonel Qaddafi announced at his country's eleventh anniversary celebrations of the revolution, in September 1980, that it and Syria had agreed to unite. Although Syria and Libya had held discussions to this end, and the Syrian prime minister was on the platform with Qaddafi, the Syrians appeared to have been surprised by the sweeping language that Qaddafi used. A year later, no discernible progress had been made toward uniting two very disparate entities, Syria with its highly structured one-party system and Libya with a decentralized structure, in which people's bureaus substitute for government bureaucracy. In August 1981, the two leaders continued to talk of unity in meetings that brought together representatives of the Baath party and the people's bureaus for the first time in months.

Despite the lack of progress in building institutions for political unity, Syria and Libya have achieved a considerable harmony in their external relations in recent years. Qaddafi is vigorously opposed to peace with Israel such as Egypt has made, and he supports Asad's confrontations with Israel in Lebanon. Both Asad and Qaddafi support the Iranian side in the

Iraqi-Iranian war. Syria has joined Libya in the latter's association with Algeria and the People's Democratic Republic of
Yemen. The latter three states are motivated by a philosophy of
national liberation and by ideological rather than pragmatic
considerations generally; Libya and Yemen are also motivated
by extreme leftist economic attitudes. Syria fits in rather poorly
with this group ideologically, but the four share, at least for
now, common negative attitudes toward such Middle Eastern
issues as the Israeli-Egyptian treaty and Saudi oil policy.

The three also are on good terms with the USSR, a state
with which Syria has developed increasingly close relations of
late. The contrast between 1976, when the Syrians ordered
troops into Lebanon without giving any advance warning to
Soviet Premier Alexei Kosygin, who was in Damascus holding
discussions with Syrian leaders, and October 1981, when the
two states signed a treaty, is striking. It is the more so because
Syria for years resisted Russian efforts to get it to enter into a
formal treaty relationship.

THE SOVIET UNION

The variety of misfortunes, external and domestic, that has
afflicted Syria in recent years must be numbered among the
causes that led the Asad regime to sign a Friendship and
Cooperation Treaty with the USSR on October 8, 1980. Similar
to treaties made in earlier years with India, Iraq, and Egypt
(since abrogated), it provides for cooperation in political, economic, scientific, technological, cultural, and military spheres.
It does not require the USSR to come to Syria's aid if it is in
danger but provides for consultation and cooperation with the
aim of removing the threat to Syria's security. Formalizing
Syrian-Soviet ties, the treaty is the culmination of events going
back to 1955, when the USSR first supplied modest quantities of
arms to Syria. In the years since then the USSR has come to be
virtually the sole source of arms for Syria, resupplying it extensively after the losses of 1967 and 1973.

Syria was among the earliest states to receive economic aid
from the USSR under an agreement in 1957. This support and
arms aid were manifestations of a shift in Soviet policy toward

newly independent states that emerged after the death of Stalin. The USSR turned from supporting local communist parties as revolutionary instruments to building state-to-state relations with countries as the principal means to achieve political influence and eventually bring about compatible political and economic systems. The Communist party of Syria, which is among the oldest of the Arab communist parties, has since the mid-1950s limited itself to the roles of seeking legitimacy, getting accepted in the Syrian political arena, and influencing events by propaganda and example. It has not been a revolutionary party, although factions wishing to follow a revolutionary line have from time to time split off from it.

The term "state-to-state relations" is a bland one that requires spelling out. A major element in Syrian-Soviet relations has been arms supply. In the period 1955–1980, the USSR has supplied military equipment worth several billion dollars. The types include jet aircraft of increasing sophistication (the MIG-25 is the newest model), armor, artillery, air defense equipment that includes surface-to-air missiles, radar, and the like. For the past several years, more than three thousand Soviet military advisers and trainers have functioned in Syria.

The USSR and several countries of Eastern Europe are heavily involved in Syria's economic development. Some $1.8 billion in economic aid has been extended by these countries through 1980. The principal areas of this effort, which is meshed into Syria's five-year plans, are transportation, irrigation, power, and petroleum. Help in developing oil production from small fields in the northeast part of the country has made Syria a net exporter of crude oil (the Syrian fields produce oil of a type for which the country has only moderate use, but it can exchange this for types that it needs). Soviets have built the railroad linking the port of Latakia with the developing northeastern part of the country. The single biggest project was the dam on the Euphrates, begun in 1968. Its first stage was inaugurated in 1973. It is designed to bring large areas of land under irrigation, a long-term and expensive project, and to generate power.

These major activities provide openings for a host of other connections and relationships. Syria, of course, has a Soviet-

Syrian friendship society. It is the beneficiary of extensive cultural exchanges in the educational, artistic, and literary fields. There is, moreover, a constant flow of delegations between the Baath party in Syria and communist and workers' parties in Eastern Europe; these occur at virtually all levels of the parties' structures. The same phenomenon occurs between people's organizations in Syria and in the Soviet camp; it is replicated in delegations representing various government ministries. These exchanges are an important but supplementary element of contact between the two sides; from the Soviet perspective, they give the Syrians insights on the role of the party in the life of society.

The effect of such extensive contact on the long-term direction of Syrian society will only be seen in a time frame measured in decades. The Soviet camp's efforts must compete with Western influences, which have had a long head start. Syrians rejected French political guidance but accepted a substantial amount of French cultural influence. In international economic matters today, Western European states, and to a lesser extent the United States, are doing very well in Syria. Western firms are building plants to make fertilizer, paper, and furniture, among other products, and are involved as well in flood control and irrigation works and petroleum projects. Syria, like many another country, has learned that Western technology in the oil business is far superior to that of the USSR and that, if the money is available, the best job may be contracted for by competition rather by relying exclusively on one source.

Despite the treaty, Syria gives no evidence of desiring to be inextricably tied to the USSR. Less than one-fifth of its trade is with the East. Like most Middle Eastern states, it has learned that the preferred relation with the superpowers is to remain able to threaten to change patrons. The treaty is an impressive monument to Soviet diligence in pursuing relations with Damascus. But the Syrian reasons for finally agreeing to sign it were not ideological affinity with the Soviet system. The Syrians are too pragmatic for that. Serious domestic troubles, near isolation in the Arab world, and the need to ensure a flow of arms all played their part.

President Asad arriving in Moscow to sign the Soviet-Syrian Treaty, Oct. 8, 1980. The Boeing 727 of Syrian Airlines shows the country's continuing commercial links with the West. (Photo courtesy of United Press International, Inc.)

THE INDUSTRIAL COUNTRIES

Relations with the countries of the industrial world are important to Syria. About one-half of its trade is with these countries, primarily those of Western Europe. Syria provides oil and agricultural products and purchases the goods and services it wishes to have to build a modern industrial economy. Neither its Arab neighbors nor the countries of the developing world are in a position to supply these items, although money from the oil-rich states does help Syria to purchase them. Curiously, despite the colonial relations that prevailed in the past, Syria feels relatively free in its relations with the European states. None is in a position to exert its will over Syria against the latter's desires. Some even offer a degree of ideological affinity, something strikingly true of the socialist administration of François Mitterand in France, which has moved rapidly to capitalize on France's reputation as a friend of the Arabs, which dates from the 1960s, and on its socialist credentials. Syria was among the first states to be visited by Mitterand's foreign minister in 1981.

In addition to recognizing their value as trading partners and aids in Syria's development, the Asad regime values the industrial states for their positions on the key issue of Israel. Several of the major European states, although allies of the United States, differ with Washington on the best policy to pursue in regard to Israel. They have offered suggestions that are on occasion closer to Syrian views than those of the United States. From Damascus's perspective, they could in time sway the latter in a direction favorable to Syria's wishes.

With the United States, Syria's relations have ranged from nonexistent in the period just after the 1967 Arab-Israeli war to fairly cordial in the mid-1970s. Kissinger arranged in 1974 for Syria to regain some of the land it lost in 1967, and that effort, of course, was welcome. American support for Sadat's peace efforts with Israel signaled a downturn in these ties. Damascus recognizes the power that the United States wields in the area; although it took pains to appear hostile to the American intermediary's efforts concerning Lebanon in the spring and summer of 1981, its support for the elements of the compromise that he helped arrange were essential to bring off the cease-fire agreement discussed above.

All in all, Syria's external affairs in the 1970s must be counted as something well short of successful. Although its horizons are limited—it does not aspire to a major leadership role among Arabs, and it is not a prominent Third World state—it has not managed either to keep on good relations with its neighbors or to bend them, however, unwillingly, to its desires. Much of the reason for this stage of affairs lies in areas well outside Syria's control. Israel has very firm ideas of what its security requirements demand; these requirements involve it almost constantly in Lebanese and Palestinian affairs in ways that run exactly counter to Syria's desiderata. Other Arab states have interests in geographic Syria; some may coincide with those of Damascus, but all of them never do. These states put resources into the area in the form of money, arms, and political support, resources that all too frequently act as impediments to Syrian policies. The net result is a Syria frustrated at its low level of achievement in the region immediately surrounding it and lacking consistent allies who might help it raise the success rate a little. Certainly the new relationship with the USSR, symbolized by the treaty of October 1980, is likely to be of marginal assistance at best.

Yet, for some years, Syria will remain an associate of the Arab states closest to the USSR; the People's Democratic Republic of Yemen, with an avowedly Marxist government; Libya, possessed of an enormous stockpile of Soviet-supplied weaponry; the PLO, which is feeling increasingly hemmed in by the more powerful Arab states; and the most "normal" of the lot, Algeria. In time, events will bring about a change in this lineup, if past performance is any indication. Some of the possible events are discussed in the following chapter.

9

Syria in the 1980s: Some Issues

The thirty-five years of independence have been revolutionary in their impact. In government, Syrians have experimented with parliamentary democracy, military dictatorship, single-party rule, and indirect military control. A combination of the last two has been in effect since the mid-1960s. For the same period an economic system in which the state is the dominant actor has prevailed. The current system has much that is positive to its credit. Compared to that of the 1950s, the current standard of living of the population is vastly better; far more Syrians have some means of influencing the administration that affects their lives and well-being; the one-party political structure has provided a measure of governmental stability unknown in earlier years.

This process of enormous change has raised a number of issues or questions to which the Syrian people must find answers. Those answers may turn out essentially to be ratification of the existing situation, or they may call for further change. In effect, the domestic question may be stated as, "Is the revolution over?" or "Is Syria's principal task to institutionalize the changes already accomplished?" Externally, the issue is whether Syria's identity is to be found within the bounds established at independence or in the broader area of geographic Syria; or, put another way, Can the Syrian Arab Republic become the dominant force in geographic Syria? Does pan-Arabism have any future appeal? As Syrians seek to frame answers, there will be stress, conflict, and violence internally and tensions abroad.

THE INTERNAL QUESTIONS

The Question of Succession

The first of the subissues into which the general category of the revolution's future must be divided is the question of who will or should govern the country. The old oligarchy is not a contender; revolution has eliminated it, and one cannot find even the sons or grandsons of the 1940s' elite in positions of influence. The Baath system is generally accepted. Most Syrians are in some way involved in it. One hundred fifty thousand party members, some hundreds of thousands in the various people's organizations ranging from young Vanguards to grizzled Peasant Union farmers, a large bureaucracy and government-employed industrial work force, and elected and appointed officials ensure that one way or another a majority of adult Syrians have a direct – and actually or potentially a beneficial – association with the regime. Half the population over the age of five knows no other form of government. Organized, non-Baathist political formations are small, show little vitality, and have little to offer their adherents.

But Syrian Baathists are displaying no more success and imagination in solving the problem of succession in a one-party system than many another authoritarian ruling party has shown. Baathists seized power in a military coup in 1963; since then little has been heard of the party's doctrine of responsible elective government, though it is still an article of the Baath constitution. The regionalist faction ousted its competitors in 1966 in a bloody coup. Asad used the threat of force to remove an opposing faction in 1970. In the years since, he has ensured, by employing a 1960s change in the party's internal operating rules that allows for most party commands to be appointed by the next one up the organizational ladder, that people loyal to him are in control of the civilian and military party structure. He permits argument and discussion; the 1980 Regional Party Congress was notable for the wide-ranging and free-swinging discussion of the regime's problems by the 750 delegates. And the Congress made rather sweeping changes in the makeup of the Regional Command. These changes were made with Asad's concurrence, not against his wishes.

Yet, though it is clear that the popularity of and level of general support for Asad and his regime has declined substantially in the past several years, no person or movement has emerged as a serious challenger to him. Relying on long-time close associates, on his relatives, and on newly rising supporters, he maintains tight control. The regime's monopoly of armed force is always in the background. It has been used to quell disturbances and violent manifestations of discontent in recent years, notably in Aleppo early in 1980 and in Hama in 1982. This ability, and willingness when necessary, to use force to suppress dissent may work for a long time. It does not, however, deal with the causes of discontent focused on the regime.

Sources of Dissatisfaction
with the Asad Government

There are half a dozen chief causes of discontent. Leaving aside individual grievances, which may indeed be strong enough for a person to turn to opposition but which cannot readily be categorized, the causes are these. First, the fact that Syria is governed by men from the provinces, from rural backgrounds, sits poorly with city people, who had become accustomed over the centuries to being the dominant political, social, and economic actors in the country. Even though the former "notable" families who led the society are displaced, smaller merchants and their clients are vehement in their objection to the concentration of development funds on the provinces and to the flood of people from the provinces crowding the cities, pushing into the universities, and occupying the top positions. The rural people themselves have strong memories of being exploited by the city dwellers and are enjoying their time in the sun. In city folks' eyes, they are not only usurpers but unsophisticated ones at that, unworthy to govern.

That these rural people include a high, and very visible, proportion of Alawis is a second cause of discontent. They are looked on as a group that accepted close ties with and a special status under the French. In the judgment of the strictest of

Muslim traditionalists, Alawis are not Muslims, but heretics. Even though Syria's Muslim religious leaders raised no objection to Hafiz al-Asad's serving as president, an office that under the constitution must be held by a Muslim, most of the violent opposition to the regime, expressed (as mentioned above) in the assassination of at least three hundred Alawi officials and professional men in the past five years, is carried out by persons acting or claiming to act for Sunni Muslim religious motives. Their activity is exclusively in the cities, where sectarian activists are more likely to find other persons unhappy with the regime for their own reasons and to draw support from them. This was the case in the Hama uprising of February 1982.

Persons who might not share the Muslim activists' sentiments are, however, unhappy with the regime for a third reason, also associated with its Alawi component. That is the corruption and abuse of the perquisites of office by many of the president's associates and supporters. A certain amount of such activity is expected in Middle Eastern society, particularly when the person availing himself of the privilege shows social responsibility by providing appropriate largesse to less fortunate people. In isolation, this abuse is rarely sufficient cause for resentment to take on vigorous proportions. But it can be and is being linked in the minds of some Syrians with antipathy to the rural and sectarian cast of the regime to reinforce that reason for discontent.

Fourth, less specifically caused by this regime but nonetheless a source of discontent directed at it, is the role that Damascus has assumed in the past fifteen years as *the* center of Syria. It is not merely that Damascus has grown substantially larger than Aleppo, it is that Aleppo has been downgraded to a provincial capital, the second city in the country, a town with sharply lessened influence on national policymaking. To have the headquarters of all the ministries, of the party, of the people's organizations, of everything that counts in an authoritarian society in a city that was once a rival and in some senses an inferior, grates upon the sensibilities of Aleppines. And Aleppo has long been a city in which Islam has been practiced seriously. It is not surprising that many of the largest manifestations of opposition to the regime have taken place there.

A fifth source of discontent is the string of foreign policy mishaps that have afflicted the regime in the past several years. Syria's intervention in Lebanon in 1976, though unpopular with some elements of public opinion because it initially put the Syrian army in the position of defending the Maronites, in time worked out to be fairly well accepted at home, particularly when the wheel turned and put Syria back in its customary alliance with the Palestinians and their left-wing Lebanese Muslim associates. Damascus clearly has failed to achieve the original goals of the intervention: to prevent the partition of Lebanon, to promote the establishment of a government favorable to Syria, and to forestall the creation of circumstances that would allow Israel to threaten Syrian security from the west. Israel occupies part of Lebanon, the Maronite area enjoys Israeli support, and Syrian control is limited to the north and northeast.

In the broader Arab area, Syria's fortunes are only marginally better, if that. Jordan has drifted away to ally itself with Baghdad. Syria has separated itself from the majority of Arab states by publicly associating itself with Khomeini's Iran in the latter's war with Iraq. Not many Syrians feel strongly in favor of actively supporting Iraq, but the fact that their government has permitted itself to get so far outside the general current of inter-Arab politics as to be on close terms only with Libya, the People's Democratic Republic of Yemen, and Algeria is to many further evidence of the Asad regime's ineptitude.

These several reasons have resulted in the accumulation of a substantial number of people in Syria who wish for a change either in the government's conduct or in the regime itself but who lack the capacity to accomplish that change by persuasion. The regime has indicated that it recognizes a need to accommodate at least some of the desires of the discontented, but it fears to take steps in that direction lest they result in a weakening of its own position. Probably the most harmful image an authoritarian regime can project is to be seen to be yielding to demands of those outside it. Such yielding is interpreted by potential successors as evidence that the regime's power is declining, and they are encouraged to step up opposition to it. Hence, the regime in such a position "hangs tough," hoping that if it can ride the tiger for a time, opposition forces will become discouraged and give up.

The Future of Asad

The specific question of how long Hafiz al-Asad will stay in control may be settled in the short term, perhaps in the time between the writing of this book and its publication. He, like any leader, is vulnerable to assassination. He has survived several attempts, the most recent having been in June 1980, when a member of his own guard threw a grenade at him; another guardsman took the force of the explosion. Barring assassination, efforts from outside the military-Baath complex to remove him would seem to have little chance. The concentration of physical force in the hands of the regime is too large. Indeed, such is the strength of that force that he might well be in office five or ten years from now. Predictions in such matters are hazardous, depending as they do on a great many variables, including external ones over which the Syrians could expect to have little influence.

Yet, a change of regime could occur. There are men in the present power structure who have ambitions of their own, perhaps only the negative ambition of retaining a lucrative or influential position. Should enough such men come to believe that Asad and his immediate entourage are by policies and actions putting at hazard their futures, they might be encouraged to risk combining against him. A kinship group of Alawis outside Asad's tribe could form the nucleus of a movement. Such a move would require great caution, given the regime's multiplicity of security services, and considerable good fortune to succeed. But in time, a palace revolution of that type will grow more likely.

It is, in fact, such a development that would open up as a practical possibility an answer to the question that underlies many of the manifestations of discontent discussed above. That is, is the Syrian body politic prepared to accept indefinitely being governed by members of a minority sect, one that the majority of the population has traditionally considered to be a subservient group? Numbers and tradition argue that it is not. A break in Alawi dominance through the replacement of Asad and his clan supporters by a combination of other Alawis and officers from other elements in the country could be a step in this direction. Such a step could lead to a more equitable distribution of power among the country's regions and its sects, but still under the rubric of the Baath party's philosophy.

A change of regime could be no more disruptive than was Asad's own move to the top in 1970. Or it could be violent, as was the takeover by the regionalists within the Baath party in 1966. In extreme circumstances it could amount to civil war. Much would depend on such variables as the timing, the attitudes of surrounding countries, and support from external sources.

Within Baathist philosophy, there is room for dispute over the economic structure. Domination of the economy by the state is not at issue. Within the framework of a planned economy, the present system features a pragmatic approach to problem areas. But the economy is plagued by inflation and heavily dependent on infusion of foreign aid, and economic ills are a negative factor in the regime's position. A move in the direction of greater centralization could accompany political change, depending, among other factors, on the attitudes of new people in the power structure and on overall economic performance.

The Place of Religion in Government

Over the next generation or so, Syrians will come to grips with a fundamental issue: whether secularism as the guiding political philosophy will permanently replace sectarianism. The Baath's secular doctrine, that religion is essentially a personal matter, has run in harmony with economic and social modernization. An increasingly complex economy supports this doctrine; technical qualification is more important to the effective performance of many jobs than are family ties. A large number of Syrians have in practice accepted this philosophy over the years. However, the modernization process sets up strains in any society, and when they appear there often appear with them movements that argue that a return to the former values and methods is in order.

Such a response has cropped up in much of the Arab

world; it is often referred to as "Islamic resurgence." It should be stressed, however, that there is far more than blind reaction to foreign innovation in the growth of public Islamic practice in such countries as Jordan, Egypt, and Syria. In Syria, the militant opposition to Asad's regime is characterized by the regime as the Muslim Brotherhood. This is an umbrella term that in reality covers a number of groups, the most extreme of which wish to impose a stricter code of Islamic practice than the one that prevailed even two or three generations ago. The appeal of these groups has so far been limited. The National Alliance for the Liberation of Syria, heavily influenced by men holding such Muslim religious ideas, is new and has no record by which its potential may be judged. But there are many gradations between a totally secular society and a strict Islamic one, and Syrians are in the process of choosing where their country should fall along the spectrum. The tension that this process engenders will affect Syrian politics and society for a long time.

The possible ways that the present discontent with the Syrian leadership might play itself out are, if not legion, certainly many. They point in the 1980s to the likelihood that Syria will undergo a period of instability as its people attempt to work out the next stage of the process that has engaged them for several decades. The several issues discussed above will affect the process in complex ways. It may be difficult to determine if a given person supports the system because he is a secularist or a provincial or an Alawi or a Baath ideologue or some combination of these. Likewise, a person might oppose the system because he is a practicing Muslim or because he is a city type or because he feels excluded in some way from the power structure. Simplistic categorization of opposition or establishment is sure to be misleading.

THE EXTERNAL QUESTIONS

How Syria is to fit into the region is equally problematic. There are still people alive who recall the time when to be a Syrian meant to be an Arab-speaking inhabitant of geographic Syria. The designations "Lebanese," "Jordanian," or "Palestinian" were not in use seventy-five years ago. Immigrants to the

United States from geographic Syria before World War I called themselves Syrians. Even this name was a subsidiary identification to the broad one of Ottoman subject or the specific one of religious-sect member. During the first two decades of this century, to identify oneself as an Arab rather than as a citizen of the Ottoman state became attractive to many. But Arabism was not a term for Syrians only. In the minds of its advocates it was meant to embrace all who spoke Arabic as their first tongue and for whom the experience of Islam was an essential element. This formulation was designed to include Christians in the pan-Arab movement. But for many of the Christian inhabitants of geographic Syria, Arabism was but another term for Islam. They feared being submerged in an Islamic sea. Muslims in geographic Syria had no such problems, whether they were majority Sunnis or were from one of the smaller sects. Druze practice calls for adapting to the political reality of the time and place (which is why Druzes did not flee with the rest of the population when the Israelis occupied the Golan in 1967), and Druzes could easily be both particularist and pan-Arabist simultaneously.

The division of geographic Syria into British and French mandated areas and then the division of the French portion into Lebanon and the states of Damascus, of Aleppo, of the Alawis, and of the Druzes required the inhabitants to think of themselves in new terms. That they were no longer Ottoman subjects did not trouble them, especially as the Ottoman state had been succeeded by the nationalist Turkish Republic. But they could not be Syrians in the old geographic sense. For some, the new designations fitted with their deepest desires. Most Maronites identified with Lebanon as *their* state; most still do, the civil war in Lebanon being, in their view, a defense of their need to live in a state run by Christians. The downtrodden Alawi peasants seem initially to have welcomed French protection as offering potential improvement over the exploitation they had suffered under Ottoman rule. Muslims incorporated into Lebanon—the enlarged "Grand Liban" referred to in Chapter 5—were not enthusiastic about it. And agitation by their predominantly Muslim populations quickly forced France to rejoin Aleppo and Damascus into one state.

Practicality dictated to the leading elements in the Syrian portion of the French mandated territory that getting the Syrian heartland plus the associated states of the Alawis and Druzes free of French control should have first priority. Those who led the struggle came to see during the course of it that the proper focus of their political endeavor was that area that became the Syrian Arab Republic. Lebanon remained a matter of close concern, and the political leaders of the two states at times worked collaboratively in their effort to gain independence from France. The pan-Arabism that grew in Syria during the period of the struggle for independence was popular with intellectuals, students, and professional men. It won the verbal support but not the wholehearted commitment of the political leaders. These men governed Syria from independence until 1958, and they fundamentally accepted the Syrian state within the boundaries the French left for it in 1946. When union with Egypt came in 1958, it "represented the destruction of the independence for which they had struggled all their lives."[9]

Other among their countrymen accepted the argument that unity erasing artificial boundaries imposed on Arabs by foreign powers would do much, if not everything, to solve Arab problems. Such people often shifted their allegiance and their emotional identity from their sect, their clan, or their town directly to the Arab nation, bypassing any allegiance to the Syrian state in the process. They were part, albeit a very important part, of a movement that had adherents in other Arab states. Syrian pan-Arabists reached the pinnacle of their success with the formation of the United Arab Republic. The influence of the movement peaked in the Arab world during the period of the UAR, and the failure of the experiment left many without a political focus.

In Syria the failure of the experiment in unity had several consequences for the issue of Syria's identity. The power of the traditional leadership was destroyed in the course of five years. Advocates of unity lost credibility and influence; the majority of the Baathists ousted in 1966 were still strong pan-Arabists. Those who succeeded them concentrated on the Syrian region. In one respect, they reverted to the sectarian identity of Ottoman days: Syria's leaders have been predominantly Alawi for more than a decade. In another way, however, they have been leaders of the Syrian Arab Republic, working for it, not using it on behalf of the Alawi minority.

Curiously, for men whose focus is the Syrian Arab Republic, these leaders have three times involved Syria in unity schemes – in 1971 with Egypt and Libya, in 1978 with Iraq, and in 1980 with Libya. Each effort, however, though presented in classic, pan-Arab terms, has had a nonunion purpose (see Chapter 8). The Syrian participation in all three has lacked vitality. The words of the declarations of intent to unite have been devoid of underlying substance. None of the three attempts has moved beyond the stage of committees whose missions have been to explore modalities and structures that might be acceptable to the participants.

These same rulers, however, have taken a stronger role in geographic Syria than did any of their predecessors. This active role has involved Syria deeply in the affairs of its neighbors in this area. The post-1965 regionalist leaders have strongly supported the Palestinians in their efforts to recover at least some portion of their heritage in Palestine. This support has been given at times in the service of ideology and more recently has been provided with the realization that Syria has little hope of establishing a lasting modus vivendi with Israel if the minimum of Palestinian desires is not accommodated. In furtherance of Damascus's interests in its neighbors' affairs, Syria has fought two wars with Israel since the regionalists took power. Its troops have aided Palestinians in Jordan and have been in Lebanon for the past six years.

The unhappy course of events in Lebanon since the outbreak of civil war in that country in 1975 has called into question the arrangements made by France decades ago. Damascus is only one of the actors in that unfortunate situation, which is inextricably bound up in the Arab-Israeli issue. Various Lebanese groups are challenging or defending the sectarian form of government set up in the 1940s. Palestinians, although determined to keep pressure on Israel, have lost the struggle to maintain freedom of action there, in the only country bordering on Israel where they had any mobility at all. Israel, resisting such Palestinian efforts, pays and arms Christian-led forces in a zone along its border and has for some years supported Maronite militias in the Maronite heartland; in the wake of its invasion, Israeli spokesmen are talking of the need for Israel to assure the survival of Christian Lebanon. Egypt, Libya, and Iraq have aided factions allied to them in conflict.

In Lebanon, the several communities have looked to their separate interests rather than give support to the nominal Lebanese administration. In practice, the country has been partitioned for several years. Syrians controlled the central valley; their Palestinian and Muslim allies controlled half of Beirut and much of the south; Maronites, dominated by the Phalange party, ran their traditional heartland; smaller private armies controlled other pieces of territory. The June 1982 Israeli invasion altered this political map. The Syrians hold less territory, the Maronites more, and the National Movement almost nothing. Nonetheless, the losers are not powerless. The efforts of Bashir Gemayel to reconstitute, with Israeli help, the Maronite-dominated state of the past will run into fierce opposition from many quarters in Lebanon and abroad. A new form of de facto partition could easily result. Should the division of the country persist, it would constitute a major breach in the post–World War I map-making and country-making carried out by the victorious allies.

Overturning even a part of the arrangements made by France under the mandate threatens to open Pandora's box. Such a development not only would result in a Maronite state linked to Israel, but it would also legitimize Damascus's role in geographic Syria outside the boundaries of the Syrian Arab Republic. It would thus encourage Syrian involvement in Jordan. It would add many complications to the task of achieving a settlement between Israel and its northern and eastern neighbors. In terms of Syria's identity, it would make less likely the possibility that Syrians would in years ahead restrict their political horizons only to the Republic. These are, no doubt, extreme speculations. They serve, however, to illustrate the point that Syria's future is not fixed. They indicate further that failure in actions undertaken outside the country could be the catalyst that would bring about the next change in the country's administration.

Subsumed in the overarching issues of the future of the revolutionary process in Syria and the proper bounds of the Syrian dominion are other issues. The first is that of Syrian relations with Israel. Of necessity, Israel will remain a major preoccupation. At least until some form of settlement is worked out, Syria will feel compelled to maintain large and expensive armed forces. Syria is markedly inferior to Israel in military terms, and it has no prospect of significant military support from its Arab associates. Leaving aside the present bad relations with Egypt, Jordan, and Iraq, which will in time be ameliorated, Syria cannot expect assistance from any of them. Egypt is excluded because of its peace treaty, Iraq because it will be facing east to deal with the consequences of its invasion of Iran for many years, Jordan because of its small size and relative military weakness. Damascus will be forced to practice caution, avoiding direct conflict with the Israelis. It will be constantly inhibited by the realization that miscalculation could lead to the very hostilities that it could have no realistic expectation of winning.

But to address the Syrian-Israeli question solely in bilateral terms is misleading. The three outstanding issues between Israel and its Arab neighbors – Lebanon, the Golan Heights, and the Palestinians – are linked. Syria is involved in all three. No one can be settled without making arrangements for the other two. In theory Syria could reach a Golan settlement with Israel. But alone this settlement would not extract either party from support of its clients in Lebanon. Nor would it get the Palestinians out of Damascus or Lebanon. A West Bank arrangement alone would do no better. Barring heroic measures and extraordinary luck, Syria will be at loggerheads with Israel for the foreseeable future.

The need to face Israel militarily will condition Syria's relations with the major powers. The USSR is likely to remain Syria's principal, if not sole, weapons supplier, as the Syrians need arms; are used to Soviet equipment, doctrine, and training; and would find it hard to pay for arms from others. At the same time, commercial and cultural pulls to the West will remain strong. In these areas there is likely to be considerable competition, as the Soviets attempt to capitalize on the military and economic aid they supply and on the access to Syrian institutions provided by the cultural and political ties that are a feature of the relationship between the two.

Its status in the Arab world remains important to Syria. With a centuries-long history of being the object of various neighbors' acquisitive instincts behind it, the modern Republic's search for an independent posture will go on. This posture clearly has not yet been found, as the swing from unity with Egypt to isolation among the Arab states in a span of six years in the 1960s demonstrates. Damascus's effort to be at once independent, a part of the Arab community, and the dominant force in its hinterland of geographic Syria is sure to complicate its life marvelously in the years ahead. Success may elude it in these efforts, but the imperatives that spring from the past, from its neighbors' interests, and from its own sense of nationhood leave Syria no choice but to try.

Notes

1. Radio Damascus (Foreign Broadcast Information Service), January 28, 1981.

2. Article 12 of the Constitution of the Baath party, translated in Sylvia Haim, ed., *Arab Nationalism: An Anthology* (California Library Reprint Series) (Berkeley: University of California Press, 1974).

3. A. H. Hourani, *Syria and Lebanon; A Political Essay* (London: Oxford University Press, 1954), p. 54.

4. A good description of how this enlarged state came about is in Elie Kedourie, "Lebanon: The Perils of Independence," *The Washington Review of Strategic and International Studies 1* (July 1978):84–89.

5. The material on the Hama events and subsequent matters is drawn from John F. Devlin, "Syria Since the Egyptian-Israeli Peace Treaty," a paper presented May 2, 1982, at a conference on the Middle East since the Treaty. The conference was sponsored by Baltimore Hebrew College.

6. Edith Penrose and E. F. Penrose, *Iraq: International Relations and National Development* (London: Ernest Benn and Associates, 1978), p. 253.

7. Patrick Seale, *The Struggle for Syria: A Study in Post-war Arab Politics, 1945–1958* (London: Oxford University Press, 1965).

8. Walid Khalidi, *Conflict and Violence in Lebanon: Confrontation in the Middle East*, Harvard Studies in International Affairs, No. 38 (Cambridge, Mass.: Harvard University Press, 1979), is the best available analysis of the Lebanese crisis, its actors, and the interplay among them.

9. Patrick Seale, *The Struggle for Syria*, p. 324.

Suggested Readings

This short bibliography will introduce the interested reader to the more important works dealing with modern Syria.

Books

The current literature is not large. The works listed below offer more detail on the topics and periods mentioned.

Devlin, John F. *The Ba'th Party: A History from Its Origins to 1966.* Stanford, Calif.: Hoover Institution Press, 1976.

Khalidi, Walid. *Conflict and Violence in Lebanon: Confrontation in the Middle East.* Cambridge, Mass.: Harvard University Press, 1979.

Longrigg, Stephen H. *Syria and Lebanon Under French Mandate.* London: Oxford University Press, 1958.

Rabinovich, Itamar. *Syria Under the Ba'th, 1963–1966: The Army-Party Symbiosis.* Jerusalem: Israel Universities Press, 1972.

Seale, Patrick. *The Struggle for Syria: A Study in Post-war Arab Politics, 1945–1958.* London: Oxford University Press, 1965.

Torrey, Gordon H. *Syrian Politics and the Military (1945–1958).* Columbus, Ohio: Ohio State University Press, 1964.

Van Dam, Nikolaos. *The Struggle for Power in Syria: Sectarianism, Regionalism and Tribalism in Politics, 1961–1980.* Second edition. London: Croom Helm, 1981.

Articles

For the inner workings of the contemporary Syrian system, the following sources are instructive.

Batatu, Hanna. "Some Observations on the Social Roots of Syria's Ruling Military Group and the Causes for Its Dominance." *Middle*

East Journal 35 (1981):331–344.

Hinnebusch, Raymond A. "Local Politics in Syria: Organization and Mobilization in Four Village Cases." *Middle East Journal* 30 (1976):1–24.

―――. "Political Recruitment and Socialization in Syria: The Case of the Revolutionary Youth Federation." *International Journal of Middle East Studies* 11 (1980):143–174.

Springborg, Robert. "Baathism in Practice: Agriculture, Politics and Political Culture in Syria and Iraq." *Middle Eastern Studies* 17 (1981):191–209.

Van Dusen, Michael H. "Syria: Downfall of a Traditional Elite." In *Political Elites and Political Development in the Middle East*, edited by Frank Tachau, pp. 115–155. New York: Halsted, 1975.

Bibliography

There is one bibliography of recent date.

Bleaney, C. H., comp. *Modern Syria: An Introduction.* Durham, England: University of Durham, 1979.

Index

Absolutely first-rate and is indispensable to those who wish to be well informed about and to understand contemporary Syria.

—Washington Report on Middle East Affairs

Devlin succeeds in compressing a substantial amount of factual and analytic material ranging from early history to modern education, politics, and economic development.

—Choice

A concise and well-written account of Syria's political, economic, and social development by a former CIA Mideast analyst, highly recommended to anyone wishing to understand that country's present situation and future prospects.

—Foreign Service Journal

The Arab Republic of Syria, though heir to a past that reaches back into antiquity, is the result of forces and events peculiar to the twentieth century, a state whose terms of existence were established by outsiders, predominantly Europeans. In the three and a half decades since independence in 1946, Syrians have been caught up in the process of adjusting to, modifying, or overturning those terms, searching for a truly Syrian identity. The process has been convulsive: The coup d'etat was for a time a seemingly integral influence in governing the country, and Syrians have variously looked on the entire Arab world, an enlarged Syria, the present republic, their religious sect, or their district as the proper focus of political identity.

In this concise profile of Syria, John F. Devlin depicts the factors that shaped modern Syria, introducing its land, people, and culture and explaining how it moved from being the coup-prone cockpit of inter-Arab politics to the relative stability of recent years. He discusses how its political system functions, the development of its moderate socialist economy, the nation's external affairs (particularly within the Middle East), and issues for the future—the last of particular interest because Syria is in a process of change in its politics, society, and international relationships. Throughout, he provides a framework within which to understand and assess the developments in Syria in the 1980s.

John F. Devlin, a consultant and writer on the Middle East, has been a Middle Eastern analyst in the Office of National Estimates of the Central Intelligence Agency and was deputy director of the CIA's Office of Political Research from 1974 to 1976.

ISBN 0-8133-0021-5